D1608206

THE FAILURE OF DEMOCRATIC
NATION BUILDING

THE FAILURE OF DEMOCRATIC NATION BUILDING: IDEOLOGY MEETS EVOLUTION

ALBERT SOMIT
AND
STEVEN A. PETERSON

THE FAILURE OF DEMOCRATIC NATION BUILDING

First published in 2005 by
PALGRAVE MACMILLAN™
175 Fifth Avenue, New York, N.Y. 10010 and
Houndmills, Basingstoke, Hampshire, England RG21 6XS
Companies and representatives throughout the world.

PALGRAVE MACMILLAN is the global academic imprint of the Palgrave Macmillan division of St. Martin's Press, LLC and of Palgrave Macmillan Ltd. Macmillan® is a registered trademark in the United States, United Kingdom and other countries. Palgrave is a registered trademark in the European Union and other countries.

ISBN 1–4039–6781–4

Library of Congress Cataloging-in-Publication Data

Somit, Albert.
    The failure of democratic nation building : ideology meets evolution / Albert Somit and Steven A. Peterson.
        p. cm.
    Includes bibliographical references and index.
    ISBN 1–4039–6781–4
        1. Democracy. 2. Democratization. 3. United States—Foreign Relations. I. Peterson Steven A. II. Title.

JC423.S682 2005
327.73′009′015—dc22   2005049184

A catalogue record for this book is available from the British Library.

Design by Newgen Imaging Systems (P) Ltd., Chennai, India.

First edition: November 2005

10 9 8 7 6 5 4 3 2 1

Printed in the United States of America.

. . . this whole tendency to see ourselves as the center of political enlightenment and as teachers . . . strikes me as unthought-through, vainglorious, and undesirable.
George Kennan

CONTENTS

LIST OF TABLES

PREFACE

As some of our readers may recall, the disintegration of the USSR in 1991 was enthusiastically hailed in the media as an overwhelming victory for democracy. Not sharing this general euphoria, we submitted a brief article to one of this nation's leading foreign affairs journals, arguing that few if any of the "liberated" countries would become democracies in any meaningful sense of that term. After a lengthy wait, we took the liberty of asking the editor for a decision. His reply, in effect, was that although he personally agreed with our contention, he had regretfully concluded that his readers would not welcome our bleak prognosis.

Shortly thereafter, we tried again, this time sending the piece to a journal aimed primarily at natural, rather than social scientists. Here again, we encountered editorial agreement—and the same reluctance to publish a predictably unpopular point of view.

In both pieces, our basic thesis was that, contrary to the prevailing ideology, humans were genetically predisposed to authoritarian and hierarchical, rather than democratic and egalitarian, social and political structures. Even in a so-called Age of Democracy, we noted, democracies still constituted a definite minority among governments, as has been the case throughout the ages. This argument, with supporting data, was spelled out in our *Darwinism, Dominance, and Democracy: The Biological Basis of Authoritarianism* (1997), a volume that somehow escaped review by a single major political or social science journal.

Proving that we were extraordinarily slow learners, we tried again a few years later—with an even better known publishing house. This book pointed out the shortcomings of the dominant Standard Social Science Model and advanced the case for a more Darwinian conception of human nature in formulating domestic and foreign policy. Again, we apparently fell below the journals' radar screen.

We probably should have taken the hint that the times were not yet ripe for a neo-Darwinian approach to human behavior and to public policy were it not for the egregious folly of our "nation building" ventures in Afghanistan and Iraq. To borrow a famous epigram, U.S. policy has been worse than a crime; in terms of our national interest, it has been a staggering blunder. In the hope of lessening the likelihood of a repeat experience, we offer here not so much a *moral* argument (it should not be done) as a practical one—it really cannot be done.

For some twenty-five hundred years, the central issue in Western political philosophy has been "What is the nature of human nature?" Over the past half century (as we discuss in chapter 2), the newly-emergent disciplines of Primatology and Human Ethology have provided both a description of, and an explanation for, the "cross-cultural" behavioral characteristics that *Homo sapiens* so consistently manifests. The evidence amassed to date strongly suggests that Machiavelli and Hobbes were much closer to the mark than Locke and Rousseau in their strikingly different assessments of human nature generally and of *Homo politicus* in particular. This is truly an unwelcome conclusion but, as Edmund Burke advised in a pre-Darwinian era, "We cannot change the nature of things and of man, but must act upon them as best we can." Unfortunately, the wisdom of Burke's counsel has yet to be recognized either by those who set American public policy or by the great majority of our social and behavioral scientists.

Acknowledgments

We would be remiss if we did not take this opportunity to

Thank the International Political Science Association for its intellectual open-mindedness in establishing a Research Committee on Biology and Politics in 1972 and for the support (in several senses of the word) it has given the committee since then.

Express our appreciation to the *British Journal of Political Science* for making it possible for us, early on, to apprise their readers of this new way of looking at political behavior and, a couple of decades later, to describe what "biopolitics" had and had not accomplished in the interim.

Commend the American Political Science Association for so successfully shielding its readers from news of this development that the editor of a newly established sister journal could, in all innocence, hail it as a "revolutionary" movement—some 40 years after the fact.

Certainly thank Palgrave/Macmillan Senior Editor Toby Wahl and Editorial Assistant Heather Van Dusen for their unstinting help in bringing this volume to fruition.

CHAPTER ONE
INTRODUCTION

Authors who advocate predictably unpopular ideas or policies have a choice of tactics: they can risk alienating their readers at the outset or, alternatively, try to postpone and possibly lessen this danger by an indirect and circuitous statement. As the next few paragraphs make clear, we have opted for the former.

Our major thesis is that the United States should drastically curtail, if not abandon, its efforts to establish democratic governments elsewhere, that is, the so-called policy of "nation building." With rare exceptions, this policy has been unsuccessful in the past; it is unsuccessful today; and is almost surely certain to be equally unproductive in the foreseeable future.

How to justify this conclusion? Necessarily oversimplified for a one-paragraph summary, our argument runs as follows: Viable democracies (there is near-unanimous agreement) require the conjunction of very special material and social "enabling conditions." As the relative rarity of democracies and the overwhelming predominance of authoritarian governments throughout human history testify, this conjunction happens all-too infrequently. These special conditions are necessary because we (*Homo sapiens*) are social primates and evolution has endowed the social primates with an innate proclivity to hierarchically structured social and political systems and an innate tendency to dominance and submission behaviors. A species so genetically inclined is hardly promising democratic material—which is why democracies require special conditions, why even today they are a definite minority among governments, why they are so hard to establish, and why they tend to be so fragile—and why the resources expended on nation building would be more productively devoted to strengthening democracy at home rather than in trying to establish it elsewhere.

We realize that many of our readers will probably disagree with at least some of that statement. In the remaining pages of this opening chapter, therefore, we seek to persuade even the most skeptical that our criticisms of "nation building" are soundly based and our resultant policy proposals merit serious consideration.

Since we are admittedly advancing an argument that many of our readers are likely challenge, we start with a couple of purely factual statements, which, in the familiar phrase, "nobody can deny." They are

1. Throughout history, democracies have been quite rare. Even today, in the so-called Age of Democracy, they are still a minority and authoritarian polities a clear majority of existent political regimes—democratic oases, as it were, in an authoritarian desert.

2. Motivated by the familiar combinations of self-interest, altruism, and ideology, over the past 60 years the United States has spent countless billions of dollars and literally thousands of American lives in attempts to establish democratic governments elsewhere.[1] To be sure, we have not been the only country to do so. Other "Western" nations, for much the same reasons, have incurred similar, though much smaller, costs.

3. These efforts have so far been largely unsuccessful. In some countries, stable governments, let alone democracies, have yet to emerge; in many of the countries where some degree of political order has been achieved, the resulting regimes are undeniably and often unabashedly authoritarian. If we take the creation of viable democracies as our measure, it would be truly Panglossian to adjudge nation building as other than a demonstrably failed policy.

That bleak conclusion immediately gives rise to the obvious question: why has it proven so consistently difficult to establish democratic government elsewhere?[2] Needless to say, we are hardly the first persons to raise this question. It has been addressed by many social scientists and the near-unanimous answer has been that democracies require very special "enabling conditions" for their birth and survival. In fact, a sizable cottage industry has developed among scholars seeking to identify the unique conjunction of economic, social, political, and other similar conditions needed for this infrequent nativity to occur. And, while they differ on the requisite "magic mix," on one point they do concur: these enabling conditions normally take decades, often generations, to emerge and mature; they cannot be achieved by import, fiat, or external imposition, no matter how well intentioned.

We certainly agree that special conditions are required and that these conditions are not readily or often attained. This explanation is fine as far as it goes—but it does not go far enough. It stops short because most contemporary social scientists are trained in, and are committed to, the Standard Social Science Model (SSSM),[3] and the intellectual constraints of the SSSM—specifically, its unyielding insistence that human behavior "lies beyond the pale of biological explanation" (Dunbar, 1996: 8)—makes it almost impossible for its practitioners to pose, let alone answer, what we would say is the real problem—*Why does democracy require so many "special conditions" while despotism and authoritarianism can so readily take root and flourish in almost any setting?* Or, if one prefers a more currently fashionable terminology, why is authoritarianism, rather than democracy, the "default" mode of human governance? Or, to put it still more pointedly, what is it about human nature that makes authoritarianism so easy—and democracy so difficult? If we are to make any headway with this issue, we must abandon the SSSM and turn, instead, to contemporary evolutionary theory, a far more powerful explanatory system.

Folk wisdom warns that "if you may not like the answer, don't ask the question." So it is in this instance. From a neo-Darwinian perspective, these "special enabling conditions" are required because democracy (much as we would like to believe otherwise) runs counter to a powerful human behavioral tendency. Biologically speaking, humans are social primates (embarrassingly akin genetically to the chimpanzees) and, over several million years, evolution has endowed the social primates with an innate predisposition (to understate the matter) for hierarchical social and political structures. That is, social primates almost invariably form groups, troops, tribes, and societies characterized by marked individual differences in terms of status, dominance and submission, command and obedience, and by unequal access to many of the good things of life. *Sad to say, the primary reason for the prevalence of authoritarian governments, for the rarity of democracy, and for why democracy demands such special enabling conditions is to be found not in our stars but in our genes.*[4]

Understandably, this unwelcome idea almost always elicits a quite logical objection: If that is so, how then do you explain the (admittedly infrequent) appearance and survival of democracies? Part of the answer, we earlier agreed, lies in the occasional conjunction of economic, social, political enabling conditions; undoubtedly, these do play an essential role. Nonetheless, we must again turn to evolutionary theory to identify the necessary, though of itself not sufficient, human attribute that sometimes makes democracy possible.

As previously remarked, *Homo sapiens* shares with other social primates an inherent proclivity for hierarchical social and political structures. Our species, however, has also evolved a behavioral trait on which we have an unchallenged monopoly—the capacity to create, accept, and then act on the basis of beliefs and values, even when the resulting actions run counter to our innate inclinations or even our personal preferences.[5] Thus, "[W]hile every other organism we know about lives in the world as presented to them by Nature, human beings live in a world that they consciously symbolize and re-create in their own minds" (Tattersall, 2002: 78). Consequently, as one of our most distinguished biologists observes, "of all living creatures, humans are uniquely capable of disobeying those biological inclinations that whisper within them. We alone are able to say 'no' to such genetic inclinations as may predispose us to polygyny, theft, murder, etc." (Barash, 1994: 16). We have, therefore, a potential susceptibility to democratic ideas, just as we have to any other secular and religious belief. This susceptibility, as we shortly see, became an increasingly important political factor from the nineteenth century on as democratic doctrines increasingly gained popular respectability and acceptance.

Unfortunately, the capacity to create, accept, and then act on the basis of our beliefs[6] may now more often work against, rather than for, democracy. Given the basic bias of our evolutionary legacy, we (hastily: our species, not the authors or our readers) are probably more inclined to embrace authoritarian political, social, and religious ideas and values.[7] This tendency may have been strengthened of late because, for democracies to be viable, there must be a willingness to listen to, or at least tolerate, differing opinions and ideas; to compromise or amicably agree to disagree; to pursue one's objectives by peaceful means, rather than by force; to treat opponents as equally human—in sum, to play "within the rules." As our media daily report, these are not modes of behavior or values preached or practiced by the belief systems—religious fundamentalism, racism, tribalism, and rabid nationalism, to mention only some of the more virulent—which have won increasing acceptance in country after country (especially in many of the developing nations) over the past few decades.

In short, given the social primate biases of human nature, the odds against democracy have always been high. The "isms" now commanding large popular followings around the world have raised them even higher. Small wonder that nation building has made so little headway or that the outlook for the foreseeable future is hardly any more encouraging.

At the same time, the American democracy is experiencing increasingly serious economic, political, and social strains. This is, or should be, a matter of concern not only for Americans but also for all of our fellow democracies, since the "trials and tribulations of the American republic have a way of setting the agenda for other democratic societies—for better or for worse, and no doubt some of both" (Elshtain, 1995: 1). The long-term prospects of democracy worldwide, we think it fair to say, would be much better served by using our human and financial resources to strengthen democracy here at home rather than by squandering them, as is currently the case, in almost assuredly fruitless "nation building" ventures abroad.

This, in essence, is the case we try to make. Now, briefly to describe how we hope to achieve this objective.

As the reader might reasonably expect, chapter 2, entitled "Authoritarian Government: The Default Option," provides a brief summary of the key principles of neo-Darwinian theory, since this theory plays a major role in our argument against nation building. If public opinion polls are correct, more Americans believe in the Old Testament account of creation than in the Darwinian evolutionary explanation of the origins of life.[8] This is not the place, we decided, to try to persuade them otherwise. There are also those who accept evolutionary theory in principle but who, denying its applicability to humans, reject the idea that our behavior can validly be related to that of the social primates. Here, too, we felt that we should not attempt to change this belief. Our summary, therefore, has been designed for and aimed at those who, accepting evolutionary theory, are prepared to consider the possibility that our species might also be inclined to some of the behavioral tendencies common to the social primates.

In chapter 2, we describe the behavioral inclinations we share with other social primates; how and why these behavioral proclivities evolved (natural selection functioning to optimize inclusive fitness); and perhaps most important of all, the implications of an evolutionary perspective for the most central and persistent issue in Western political philosophy—the nature of political man.[9]

BUT—and the emphasis is essential—though there are many similarities, we are also profoundly different from all the other social primates. Human behavior is the product not simply of our genes but of the interaction between nature *and* nurture. We alone are capable of creating a complex culture consisting of both material objects and abstract values; we are the only species in which the values we have created are capable of overriding our strongest and most deep-seated behavioral imperatives.[10] It is this unique quality that makes it possible for democratic ideas to sometimes gain a popular following and, when this occurs in conjunction with the requisite enabling conditions, for a democracy to be born—and survive. This capability, however, also opens the way for authoritarian and antidemocratic ideas and, well, our readers can draw their own conclusions as to which have been, and continue to be, the more likely to win out.

Many Americans are unaware that, even after two victorious World Wars and a subsequent triumph over the "Evil Empire," democracies still constitute a minority among governments. There may also be many who do not realize that, on balance, nation building has so far produced little in the way of tangible results.

Accordingly, this is where we next turn. Chapter 3, entitled "What is a Democracy?: Toward a Working Definition," examines the criteria that should be—but are not always—employed to adjudge whether or not a given nation is or is not a democracy. As we point out, later in the book, few political terms have been used so elastically. Take, for instance, President Clinton's preposterously premature announcement in 1994, "We have restored democracy to Haiti." When, even the most credulous auditor might ask, have the unfortunate Haitians ever enjoyed anything remotely approaching a democracy?

Chapter 4, "Democratic Nation Building: From Concept to Operational 'Checklist,' " begins by briefly reviewing the literature to arrive at a working definition of nation building. We then look at a series of case studies to identify the activities and commitments that countries engaged in nation building must make, and the conditions that should exist if this enterprise is to succeed. Third, based on that survey, we develop a "checklist" to be utilized in deciding whether to attempt nation building in a specific state (since one's reach should exceed one's grasp, conceivably Syria or Iran). Last, we take Germany and Haiti as cases in point and examine the extent to which the proposed checklist might have predicted the outcomes of those two strikingly dissimilar nation building ventures.

Given the innate hierarchical tendency of social primates, *creating a democracy is immeasurably more difficult than establishing other forms of government*. This in essence, is the thesis of chapter 5—"Democracy: The Requisite 'Enabling Conditions'—No Small Order." There are, in fact, two types of social, economic, and political requirements that must be satisfied. The first, which relates primarily to the "target" country, we have termed "decisional requirements." The second set of conditions, which we have called "operational," (*of which a long-term commitment is a key component*) relates primarily to the country (for our purposes, the United States) making the attempt. Both sets, the data strongly suggest, must be present if nation building is to achieve its intended purposes; they take time to develop and mature, and they cannot be created "on demand," a constraint that seemingly has yet to be grasped by our policy makers.

If our basic thesis about our species' inherent inclination to hierarchical social structures is correct, it should follow that (1) contrary to what many Americans believe, democracies have not only have historically been a rare form of government but also that today, even in the so-called Age of Democracy, they continue to be a definite minority among polities; (2) with very few exceptions, nation building efforts have fallen far short of their objectives. Clearly, this is an empirical issue and chapter 6 ("Will the Real Democracies Please Stand Up?"[11]) presents the relevant statistics on the incidence of democracies in the world community today, and the relative success or failure of nation building undertakings over the past several decades. The reader will agree, we think, that the evidence supports these two contentions.

One of the world's great philosophers, still regrettably unknown to posterity, delivered her/him self of a truly immortal adage—"There ain't no such thing as a free lunch." In chapter 7, entitled "American Nation

Building, 1945–2005: Costs and Consequences," we look at the invasions of Iraq and Afghanistan in terms of the price paid by the United States[12] to date (early 2005) not only in terms of lives and dollars but also other consequences of these invasions—the deterioration of relations with many of our previous Allies, the task of almost single-handedly restoring civil order in a nation reduced to near anarchy, and the bitter divisiveness of this issue here at home. We also consider the price paid by the peoples of the occupied countries—death and destruction aside, the swift defeat and collapse of the previous regime in Iraq, whatever its horrendous defects, unleashed, possibly even sharpened, long-standing religious rivalries. These age-old animosities, now refreshed, lessen the prospects of establishing a stable government, let alone anything resembling a democracy. Whether the benefits, present or prospective, on balance outweigh the costs, readers will have to decide for themselves. While recent elections in both Afghanistan and Iraq are encouraging, elections by themselves do not ensure the development of stable, functioning democracies.

Among the most serious of these consequences of "nation building" to the United States has been the diversion of attention and resources from serious domestic problems ranging across almost the entire policy spectrum. Chapter 8, rather cryptically entitled "The Fourth Whereas," identifies four problems—the growing paralysis of our political system, poverty and inequality of wealth, the loss of social capital, and the near-total failure of our schools to teach democratic citizenship—which we regard as especially threatening to the long-term welfare of the American democracy. Our intent here is not so much to offer solutions as to convey a sense of urgency about the consequences of a continued failure to deal with these issues. However chauvinistic it may sound, we are the world's leading democracy, and our willingness and ability to address these and related problems may be the single most important factor influencing the fate of democracy around the globe.

The above discussion brings us to chapter 9, "Therefore, Be It Resolved . . .: Toward More Realistic Foreign and Domestic Policies" in which we not so much state—since these has long been adumbrated—our policy recommendations but, rather, seek to anticipate possible questions and objections. The two proposals we advance will hardly surprise anyone who followed our argument to this point: first, barring truly remarkable circumstances, abjure nation building; second, as rapidly as possible, turn our attention and, no minor matter, our resources to resolving the political, social, and economic problems that are threatening to undermine our democracy here at home. In one sense, the two policies are opposite sides of a mirror: as the events of the past few years have demonstrated, we are not very likely to succeed in the latter unless and until we adopt the former.

Intentionally or otherwise, this has been one of the most unfortunate consequences of nation building. It has diverted massive resources that should be directed, rather, to urgent domestic concerns. We need hardly have invaded Iraq for near-insoluble problems: we have an ample supply [of our own] here in the United States.

There is another weighty reason for changing course. Nation building, twenty-first century American-style, has been profoundly divisive. Our swift military destruction of the existing regimes in Afghanistan and Iraq, whatever their horrendous defects, unleashed, possibly even sharpened, long-standing religious and tribal rivalries. These age-old animosities, refreshed and renewed, both lessen the prospects of anything remotely resembling a democracy and, if political stability is to be achieved, compel a continuing investment of American resources and lives.

Our bullyboy tactics have also managed, with remarkable speed, to damage a reasonably effective diplomatic relationship with many of our previous European allies. Predictably, we were left to face, almost single-handedly, the staggering postwar task of establishing control over, and restoring civil order to, a society deeply divided along religious and ethnic lines. Perhaps worst of all, have been the repercussions here at home. The way we have gone about nation building has become a bitterly divisive issue, with the contestants angrily questioning not only their opponents' character, judgment, and honesty but also their very patriotism. Few things are as potentially dangerous to a democracy as that type of virulent partisanship.

Finally, in chapter 8, we consider some of the domestic difficulties with which the United States is—or should be—currently wrestling. The litany stretches across practically the entire policy spectrum—social, economic, fiscal, political, racial, industrial, demographic, urban, rural, agricultural, environmental, health, educational, and so on. Each of these areas has a burgeoning literature that seeks both to describe the problem(s) and to propose (often radically differing) remedies thereto. Our purpose in this chapter is not to offer our own solutions but to convey some sense of the variety and gravity of the issues with which, signs of increasing political paralysis notwithstanding, the American democracy must somehow cope. However chauvinistic it may sound, the success or failure of our democracy may be the most important single factor influencing the fate of democracy around the world.

CHAPTER TWO
AUTHORITARIAN GOVERNMENT: THE DEFAULT OPTION

Introduction

Thousands of years of recorded human history testify to an uncomfortable fact: the vast majority of humankind has lived—and continues to live—under some form of authoritarian rule. Democracies have been notably rare; most have been endangered from the moment of their birth; most have been depressingly short-lived. In brief, authoritarian government appears to be what technologically oriented readers would call the "default option" in human politics. Why? Neo-Darwinian theory, we believe, offers the single most powerful and intellectually coherent explanation.

Humans are social primates, closely akin genetically to the chimpanzees and only slightly less so to the gorillas. Working over literally millions of years, natural selection has endowed the social primates with a "predisposition" for hierarchical social structures. That is, social primate species invariably form groups, troops, tribes, and societies characterized by marked differences of individual status in terms of dominance and submission, command and obedience, and by unequal access to many of the good things in life. And these, of course, have been among the consistent characteristics of primate groups, troops, tribes, and societies, past and present.

But we should begin at the beginning. For those readers unfamiliar with evolutionary theory, the next section ("Evolutionary Theory 101") provides a brief summary of neo-Darwinism's basic tenets.

Evolutionary Theory 101

Evolution is a theory of change among living forms.[1] Whether we are looking at the evolution of horses, dogs, or humans, we see change in how the individuals within a species appear over time. Darwin's theory was based on two simple propositions: first, there is variation among creatures within any species; second, some of the variations provide survival advantage for those individuals who have them and, hence, will be selected for. As Mayr (1992: 22) puts it, "Evolution thus is merely contingent on certain processes articulated by Darwin: variation and selection."

Populations, as Malthus famously observed, tend to produce more off-spring than an environment can support. Natural selection is the process by which nature selects those individuals whose characteristics are best fit for survival in their environments. Individuals whose characteristics do not fit an environment quite so well tend to die off before reproducing or repro-duce less successfully.

Those characteristics that fit the environment and confer some survival value for the organism are termed "adaptations." The organisms best adapted to their environments are more likely to survive and to reproduce. In this sense, and in this sense alone, they are more "fit" (e.g., see Williams, 1966). Those of their offspring who inherit these adaptations are, in turn, themselves more likely to survive and reproduce. Over time, individuals within a species develop adaptations that make them increasingly more apt to enjoy reproductive success and these adaptations consequently become dominant or widespread within the species.

Assume a particular environment. Each year, two hundred young of a species are born—but this environment provides just enough food and other resources to support only one hundred of the young. Thus, about half will die. Those whose physical characteristics and behavior allow them to do better in that environment tend to be the ones who survive. They, in turn, will mature and reproduce and have their genes represented in the forth-coming generation. Evolution is not just about survival—but also about the transmission of the characteristics that further survival.

In Darwin's time and for decades thereafter, the mechanism by which adaptations were transmitted from generation to generation was unknown and evolutionary theories of the time were unable to account adequately for transmission of these adaptations. It was Gregor Mendel who described the transmission of characteristics from generation to generation, paving the way for an understanding of genetics. We now know that genes are the basic units by which characteristics are passed on from parents to offspring.

In the 1930s, biologists such as R. A. Fisher and J. B. S. Haldane and Sewall Wright began to link genetics with Darwinian natural selection. This wedding of genetics and Darwinian theory was the foundation of the modern "synthetic" theory of evolution. Two of the classic works outlin-ing the synthetic theory are by Ernst Mayr (1963) and Theodosius Dobzhansky (1951). More recently, Stephen Jay Gould has contributed his final work as a massive discourse on evolution: *The Structure of Evolutionary Theory* (2002).

An important step in applying evolutionary theory to human social behavior was taken by sociobiology—the study of the evolutionary bases of social behavior (Dawkins, 1989; Trivers, 1971; Wilson, 1975). A key concept for sociobiology is "inclusive fitness," the premise that evolution inclines living organisms to those modes of behavior most likely to maximize the number of their genes transmitted to the next generation. This can be done in two different ways: first, by passing along their genes directly, usually referred to as individual reproductive success; second, by furthering the reproductive success of their relatives, with whom they share genes. The combination of these two is termed "inclusive fitness," which encompasses both the reproductive success of an individual *and* of that individual's relatives with whom, depending upon the degree of relatedness, the individual shares more or fewer genes (see Barash, 1982; Dawkins, 1989; Wilson, 1975).[2]

Evolution and Dominance: Underlying Wellsprings of Social and Political Hierarchies

Let us illustrate the application of this perspective to social behavior, specifically with reference to dominance behavior (a striving to attain valued goods, whether food or power or shelter) and the formation of social and political hierarchies (see Somit and Peterson, 1997). Social primates display dominance behavior; they also live in hierarchical social (and in the case of our species, political) structures. Hierarchy is, in fact, one of the most pervasive and ubiquitous characteristics of human social (as well as political) organizations.

Dominance is normally defined as a relationship, among members of the same species, in which there is a high probability that the dominant animal will have preferential access to some good to which its fellow speciates also aspire.[3] The desired good may be of almost any sort—food, shelter, a reproductive partner, a territory, a preferred seating place and, by no means least of all, deference.

Two male chimpanzees, for example, may come simultaneously upon a bounty of bananas. Both are hungry and both want the bananas—but the dominant chimpanzee, either automatically or by simply a threatening gesture, will have prior access. The subordinate will eat only after the dominant has consented or finished—if any bananas remain.[4]

Dominance is achieved in a variety of ways, depending upon the species and the specific situation. Taking the animal kingdom as a whole, actual physical combat is perhaps the least common method, since it carries with it the danger of serious injury or death to one or even both of the contestants. More frequently, dominance is established by threat and display, with the smaller or less formidable looking individual yielding to a larger and more fearsome opponent. This outcome benefits both participants: for the dominant, there is no physical risk; for the subordinate, the short-term loss of status and/or access to a desired good may well be offset, in the long run, by the opportunity to grow older, stronger, and more fearsome—and perhaps eventually to reverse the relationship.

Interestingly enough, though hardly surprising from a human perspective, dominance among many social species is sometimes achieved by inheritance. Where this occurs, as with chimpanzees,[5] the offspring take on a status either equal to or just a step below the status of their mother; that is, they will normally be dominant to (most of) those chimpanzees (and their offspring) who are subordinate to her—and subordinate to those chimpanzees (and their progeny) who are superior to her. We say "normally" because it is quite possible for an ambitious son or daughter of a low-ranking mother to move markedly upward in the group's social hierarchy (i.e., to become dominant over those to whom he or she was previously subordinate) by some combination of threat, force, and alliance.

As the foregoing suggests, alliance with one or more fellow con-speciates is yet another technique for achieving a more dominant status. The making and breaking of these alliances among chimpanzees, graphically described by Frans de Waal (1989; see also Harcourt and de Waal, 1992) sometimes reaches a level of malevolent sophistication that Machiavelli himself might admire.

Darwinian theory holds that when a given behavior is consistently manifested by a species, or by a number of related species, there is probably a sound evolutionary reason for that behavior.[6] We find substantial evidence for this among baboons (Dixson, Bossi, and Wickings, 1993; Hausfater, Altmann, and Altmann, 1982; Packer et al., 1995), macaques (Bauers and Hearn, 1994; Berman, 1986; de Ruiter, van Hoof, and Scheffrahn, 1994; Paul and Kuester, 1990; Smith, 1993; Thierry, 2000) and chimpanzees (Ely, Alford, and Ferrell, 1991) to mention only a few of the primate species that have been studied (see Bernstein, 2004).

Another way in which dominance behavior affects reproductive opportunities has already been suggested. Dominance relations yield predictability. Individuals soon learn where they stand with one another with respect to access to valued resources.[7] As a consequence, there is no need constantly to dispute who is to get what, disputes that, at best, would entail repeated and possibly substantial investments of energy and, at worst, repeated risks of injury or death.

Dominance furthers predictability and predictability, in turn, benefits both the dominant and the subordinate. The former gains the desired resource (and resulting possible enhancement of inclusive fitness) at no greater cost than a possible threat or two; the subordinate, by yielding, escapes a clash that might otherwise reduce or literally end his/her reproductive possibilities.

There is yet another benefit. A society beset with continuing turmoil is not conducive to reproductive success. The more orderly mode of life generated by the type of predictability just described creates more felicitous conditions for passing one's genes along to the next generation. A stable, peaceful society is more apt to lead to individual reproductive success than one in continuing upheaval as a result of constant fighting over status and resources.

In simple, small primate societies, dominance relations usually lead to "linear" hierarchies, with each animal ranked from top (alpha) to bottom (omega). But in more complex societies, as previously mentioned, several animals may unite in an alliance or a coalition so that they wind up on top—even though some of them might otherwise rank much lower purely on the basis of dyadic (one to one, simple dominance) relations.[8] Dominance hierarchies in these societies, consequently, are not simply the sum of all dyadic relations.

However, whether a society is characterized by a linear hierarchy or by a more complex coalition structure, the net result is essentially the same in evolutionary terms. Hierarchy leads to social stability, and stability—on balance—is conducive to more successful reproduction among the members of that society. Hierarchy, an outgrowth of dominance relations among a social species, functions to enhance the likelihood that the individuals who constitute that species will optimize their inclusive fitness. The direct benefit is to the individual—but the group and, ultimately the species may itself also gain thereby.[9]

From a neo-Darwinian perspective, whether considered solely from the benefits to the individual or conceivably to the group or species, this is why hierarchical social structures evolved among social primates as a consistent and significant component of their behavioral repertoire.[10] And, as with our social primate relatives, so, too, with humans.

Hierarchy, Evolution, and Humankind

Democracies have been rare, our thesis holds, because we are genetically predisposed toward authoritarian social structures. The logic of this argument obviously requires that the same predisposition for hierarchical organizations be found operative not only in the political realm but in practically every aspect of our species' social life. The purpose of this section is to persuade—or remind—the reader that such is precisely the case. Donald Brown (1991) has collected a list of "human universals," many of which speak to a predisposition to hierarchy among humankind: Males engage in coalitional violence; Males dominate the public/political realm; Dominance/submission; Leaders; Economic inequalities; Prestige inequalities; Statuses and roles; Oligarchy.

There is something paradoxical, if not ironic, about the need to demonstrate the universality among humans of hierarchical structures embodying marked differences of status, benefits, and privilege, or of the manifold material and psychological gains and losses that are associated with these differences. Of all social phenomena, hierarchy is the most pervasive; for almost all of us, the major and minor events of our existence occur within, and are shaped by, one hierarchy or another.[11] This was true in the past; as Joseph Shepher (1987: 174) noted, it is no less the case today:

> Modern human life is basically a study in dominance hierarchies: we spend most of our waking hours in hierarchies that range from corporate industry to government administration, from supermarkets to department stores, from the elementary school to the university. Even our clubs, associations, churches, and hospitals are hierarchically organized, all displaying a wide variety of dominance systems . . . modern adolescents can hardly find a more important system to adjust to than dominance hierarchies.

Shepher's last point is especially important. If dominance hierarchies are omnipresent, so, too, are status distinctions. As might be expected of *Homo sapiens*, the social primate par excellence, these distinctions "exist in groups of whatever kind, from garden clubs, to street gangs, to orchestras with soloists and dramatic conductors, to seminaries where some are holier than others and holier than thous . . ." (Tiger, 1992: 266).[12] Randolph Nesse expressed the same idea when he observed that "it is possible to get enough food and water, for a time, at least, but no amount of social status seems enough" (1994: 343).

Even language, that transcendent tool that sets humankind apart from all other species, reflects our seemingly ineluctable tendency to create and then observe differences of rank. That is hardly surprising: According to the Noam Chomsky school of linguistics, these "deep structure" language communalities are literally rooted in the anatomical structure and physiological functioning of the human brain. Practically all languages abound in honorifics and in pronouns (*Sie, Du*, avoidance of the direct "you" in speaking to a superior, etc.,) that recognize and reinforce status distinctions; in some languages even verbs are modified for the same purpose.

Despite—or more likely because of—the manner in which hierarchy permeates our social existence, students of human behavior have been surprisingly slow to grasp its pervasiveness. The reason, according to Louis Dumont, is that "Modern man [*sic*] is virtually incapable of fully recognizing [hierarchy]. If it does force itself on his attention, he tends to eliminate it as an epiphenomenon" (1966: xvii). Dumont is probably right; it is usually very difficult to take adequate cognizance of that which is totally familiar.[13] In any event, even when its importance is recognized, we have been slow to understand hierarchy's evolutionary origins and significance.

The initial explanations for the universality of hierarchy and of status differentiations were, and by most social scientists probably still are, cast in purely sociological terms—that is, social learning, separate invention, cultural diffusion, and borrowing and imitation. Although theoretically conceivable, it is highly improbable that *social learning* can even begin adequately to account for the regularity and similarity of dominance structures and dominance-related behaviors among peoples separated by vast distances of time, space, and cultural development.[14] Instead, as Tiger and Fox argued in one of the first full-scale neo-Darwinian challenges to the long-accepted sociological wisdom (and to the SSSM),

> [I]n this business of being inferior and superior, we do not begin from scratch but rather draw on an elaborate repertoire of already programmed ways of showing those differences of status it seems we are compelled to show. The inflexible and consistent connection of all this with the way we evolved as a breeding species confirms our connection with our own prehistory. (1971: 41–42).

More recently, Benson Ginsberg—to cite only one of many other examples of the neo-Darwinian perspective[15]—has expressed the same idea, albeit more briefly and conservatively:

> All [human] groups have their dominance-deference hierarchies. Collectively and historically, such hierarchical organizations appear to be rooted in the biological nature of our species, and must, therefore, be, in part, understood in evolutionary terms[16] (1988: 1).

Obedience: Servile Handmaiden to Hierarchy

One social scientist has observed that "[T]he widespread support for royalty throughout much of human history suggests the importance of considering the complicity of subjects in their own subordination" (Schwartz, 1989: 270). True, the "subjects" are guilty of complicity—though only in the sense that they acted in compliance with one of *Homo sapiens'* preprogrammed behaviors, our "innate inclination to obey" (Eibl-Eibesfeldt, 1979: 95). Obedience is the handmaiden of hierarchy. Some individuals are dominant; others are obedient, willing to accept the dominance of those above them in the hierarchy.

As the foregoing suggests, among our species' most powerful and persistent evolutionary legacies is a readiness to give "obedience to those in authority" (Sagan and Druyan, 1992: 169), a readiness hardly conducive to either the emergence or the survival of democratic governance, a readiness evidenced by the world around us and by research findings.

Before proceeding further, though, it is imperative that we make clear just what we *are* and, maybe even more important, what we are *not* saying. Not all obedience, we certainly agree, can reasonably be attributed solely to an evolutionarily derived predisposition. Some acts of obedience are no doubt voluntary in that we obey a law or a command because we think the action requested is right, moral, or desirable: possessing freedom of choice, we would take the same action, even if not commanded to do so.

In other instances, obedience is most sensibly explained in terms of threat and force.[17] Individuals, groups, and sometimes entire populations obey because they have sound reason to fear the consequences of disobedience. It may well be that, as we are often reassured, "[S]tark coercion, unsupported by other devices, is usually unsuccessful over long periods of time" (Wilkinson, 1969: 8). But even the most coercive regimes rarely rely on force "unsupported by other devices"; in any event, this long-term consolation may be inadequate incentive to risk paying the price of disobedience in the short run.

Last, obedience may flow simply from social conditioning and established habit, keeping in mind that this is a teaching, as we will see, for which evolution has made us extraordinarily adept pupils. From early infancy on, we learn to obey because "the school, the family, the workplace, the church or synagogue, athletics—all of these institutions function, more or less explicitly, on the basis of obedience to authority." The end result is that "the average individual becomes extremely well versed in the act of obedience" (Miller, 1986: 223). Given this habituation, no wonder that "the habit of obedience dies hard" (Tiger and Fox, 1971: 29).[18]

Among humans, then, obedience springs from diverse sources and it would be manifestly erroneous to attribute all obedience entirely to our evolutionary heritage. We believe, however, that our inherent tendency to submit provides the most powerful, *but by no means only*, explanation for what Nobel Laureate Herbert Simon (1990: 1665) has euphemistically termed "human docility."

We noted earlier that dominance and hierarchy can reduce intraspecific violence (and so optimize the inclusive fitness of both dominants and subordinates). There must also concurrently evolve, in Eibl-Eibesfeldt's phrase, "a disposition to accept subordination and obedience" (1989: 309). In short, however repugnant the idea, natural selection has endowed us with "a readiness to comply with a submissive role" (van der Molen, 1990: 63).

Acts of obedience can be of two sorts. In one, the organism does something that it would prefer not to do; in the other, the organism refrains from doing something that, left to its own choices, it would prefer to do. An example of the former would be a situation in which a subordinate chimpanzee gives up a desirable resting place to a dominant; in the latter, it refrains from copulating with a receptive female because of the threat, explicit or implicit, of a dominant.

In the case of chimpanzees—or members of any other social species—obedience is rendered to more dominant fellow speciates, that is, those who occupy a superior place in the group's *social* hierarchy. Humans, to be sure, live in many hierarchies. In this discussion, though, we are concerned only with *political* obedience, that is, actions taken by subordinates in response to the commands, again implicit or explicit, of those above them in the political (or sometimes military) hierarchy. So long as this hierarchy is perceived as "legitimate"[19] our genetic tendency is to obey. As Kelman and Hamilton stress, one "striking phenomenon of hierarchies of authority . . . is the readiness of citizens to accept orders unquestioningly . . . even when obedience entails enormous personal sacrifices or the commitment of actions that, under other circumstances, they would consider morally reprehensible" (1989: 137). Robin Dunbar (1996: 143) echoes this when he states that "the one feature of human behavior that is *really* difficult to explain: our extraordinary willingness to subject ourselves to someone else's will. . . ."

Obedience is thus a behavioral correlate of dominance and hierarchy.[20] If inclusive fitness is to be optimized, a social species must evolve all three behaviors—dominance relations, hierarchical social systems, and obedience. All three, surely, are characteristic of *Homo sapiens*. Not surprisingly, this disposition or inclination can be discerned at a very youthful age: According to Stayton et al., the "earliest manifestation of obedience in an infant appears in the final first quarter of the first year of life" (1971: 1058). Discussing similar results achieved with slightly older children, they comment that

> These findings cannot be predicted from models of socialization which assume that special intervention is necessary to modify otherwise asocial tendencies of children. Clearly, these findings require a theory that assumes that an infant is initially inclined to be social and [somewhat later] ready to obey those persons who are most significant in his [*sic*] social environment.

It is possible, of course, to agree that humans consistently manifest these behaviors and yet to still deny that they have a *genetic* basis. This view is sometimes encountered even within the neo-Darwinian camp among those who accept evolutionary theory as it applies to all *other* species but who, nonetheless, are convinced that "human beings in their social behavior, alone, have succeeded in escaping biology" (Degler, 1991: viii). Such a position is logically tenable if one believes that there is a vast, unbridgeable gap between all other forms of life, including the great apes, and ourselves.

The contention that biology cannot and does not provide an acceptable explanation for human behavior is more commonly encountered, however, among those who see behavior as primarily, if not totally, determined by "learning." This, in fact, was the overwhelmingly prevailing wisdom in American social and behavioral sciences until at least the 1950s[21]—and, though now gradually losing adherents, it undoubtedly remains the majority position today.

With regard to obedience, then, psychologists, social psychologists, and other behavioral scientists who are "psychologically" oriented almost invariably explain both history and experimental results[22] involving obedience in terms of learning and "socialization" rather than as having some genetic basis. Ralf Dahrendorf, one of Europe's preeminent social scientists, captured both the essence of this belief—and quite unintentionally the underlying emotional dynamics—when he assured his colleagues that "our body is not the 'real' us, [and] that biological concepts and theories cannot affect the integrity of our individuality" (1968: 20).

Since nothing is to be gained by rehashing here the "nature vs. nurture"[23] dispute, two questions must suffice as counterarguments. First, does not the near-universality of obedience point to an underlying "human nature" as a major, though not necessarily exclusive operative influence? Second, if obedience is simply learned, how other than in terms of genetic "preprogramming" can we explain the remarkable readiness of *Homo sapiens* to acquire and exhibit this behavior across the ages and around the world?

In addition, a large body of experimental evidence testifies strongly to our tendency to obey. Arguably, the most famous (or infamous, depending upon one's viewpoint) research on "obedience to authority" were the experiments conducted by Stanley Milgram between 1960 and 1963. Since almost anyone likely to read this book is probably already familiar with his work, it needs be only briefly discussed here.

What will "normal" people do, Milgram sought to ascertain, when ordered to impose electric shocks of increasing severity (and painfulness) on another person?[24] Forty men, representing a variety of professions, were recruited as subjects via mail and newspaper solicitation. These 40 volunteers were instructed to play the role of "teachers" in the experimental situation; members of Milgram's team were given the ostensible role of "learners."

Each teacher was told to read a series of word pairs to the learners and then to read the first word of a pair and four possible associations. The learners were to indicate which of the four associations had in fact been paired with the first. The instructions authorized the teachers to punish the learners for each error of recall by pressing a lever on a shock generator.

The shock generator operated by the teachers had a panel with 30 levers; the levers (the teachers were informed) administered electrical shocks to the learners in strengths ranging from 15 to 450 volts, as indicated on each lever. So that there would be no ambiguity as to the strength of the shock, many of the levers also had an additional marking, starting with "Slight Shock" and going to "Very Strong Shock," "Intense Shock," "Extreme Intensity Shock," and finally "Danger: Severe Shock." These last two levers were further marked "XXX." As the experiment was designed, the teachers could also hear (but not see) the learners (presumably) pounding on the wall in pain as the shock level (presumably) increased and became progressively more agonizing.

In those instances where a teacher seemed reluctant to administer a shock, the experimenter would respond with one of four "prods" of increasing urgency—(1) "Please continue" or "please go on"; (2) "The experiment requires that you continue"; (3) "It is absolutely essential that you continue"; and (4) "You have no other choice, you must go on."

The results? Contrary to the expectations of three groups (including 39 psychiatrists) asked to predict the probable behaviors, and to Milgram's surprise and dismay, 26 of the 40 subjects obeyed when, in the course of the experiment, they were ordered to press the 450 volt ("XXX Danger: Extreme Intensity Shock") lever. True, some of them were clearly reluctant; many, according to Milgram, "were observed to sweat, tremble, stutter, bite their lips, groan, and dig their fingernails into their flesh" (1974: 375). Many hesitated, many seemed disturbed—*but they obeyed*.

Milgram himself was appalled by the outcome of his experiment. The "chief finding" and "the fact most urgently demanding explanation," he wrote, "is the extreme willingness of adults to go to almost any lengths on the command of an authority . . ." (1974: 14). How, then, to explain this willingness to obey?

In Milgram's opinion, the subjects obeyed because "we are born with a *potential* for obedience, which then interacts with the influence of society to produce the obedient man. In this sense, the capacity for obedience is like the capacity for language: "certain highly specific mental structures must be present . . ." (1974: 125). That innate capacity for obedience, he ruefully concluded, "is the fatal flaw that nature has designed into us, and which in the long run gives our species only a modest chance of survival" (1974: 188).[25]

Milgram was not the first psychologist to explore obedience to command and social pressure. Jerome Frank (1944) had previously demonstrated that an experimenter could lead subjects to consume a nauseating quantity of soda crackers. Earlier, Muzafer Sherif (1936) had shown that judgments (regarding a point of light in a darkened laboratory) were readily swayed by the (apparently differing) opinions of others. And, of course, Solomon Asch, for whom Milgram had once served as an assistant, presented convincing evidence (1956) that peer pressure could lead the subjects to make "glaring errors on an unambiguous line-estimation problem" (Miller, 1986: 16).

As might be expected, Milgram's work provoked not only a torrent of comments but also inspired many attempts to replicate—or possibly contradict—his finding. David Mantell (1971) essentially duplicated Milgram's experiment, requiring the subjects to administer electrical shocks, and so on. Although Mantell later described the laboratory setting in which the subjects performed as "senseless," the subjects nonetheless obeyed.

Changing the research design to provide a nonhuman "victim," Sheridan and King (1972) instructed their subjects, as part of a putative study of canine visual discrimination, to shock a "cute, fluffy puppy." More than half of the male subjects and, curiously enough, 100 percent of the female subjects, were "maximally obedient." Kilham and Mann (1974) further varied the experiment by having their subjects transmit to someone else, rather than personally execute, the orders to shock the (in this instance, a human) "learner." Again, the prevailing response was obedience—even up to the fictitious 450 volt level. And, in a more recent Dutch version of the Milgram format, the overwhelming majority of subjects complied as instructed (Meeus and Raaijmakers, 1985).

Obedience experimentation has not been limited to adults. Slightly modifying Milgram's paradigm, Shanab and Yahya (1978) tested the willingness of Jordanian public school students to follow commands. Almost three-quarters of those involved obeyed up to and including the highest shock level. When essentially the same experiment was undertaken with college students, they found the results to be much the same.

John Martin and his associates introduced an interesting modification. There, the subjects (13- and 14-year-old male schoolchildren) were ordered to carry out tasks (listening to sounds at increasingly high frequencies) that were "clearly and explicitly described as potentially harmful to themselves" (1976: 346). Some 95 percent turned the dial to the level which, they had been told, carried with it the danger of a 20 percent possible hearing loss; over half of them then went on to the maximum level.

The above constitute a fairly representative, albeit by no means complete list of the "obedience experiments" undertaken to date. There is no need to belabor the point: no matter how the experiments differed in detail and design, the results were almost always the same—the subjects obeyed.

A Small Darwinian Window for Democracy

What about the observation that democracies *do* appear from time to time and that, happily, some *do* survive? There were, after all, maybe 50 glorious democratic years in Athens and, after a lengthy interval, a century or so of democratic grandeur in Rome. Then, after a hiatus of more than a millennium and a half,[26] there once again emerged another democracy in the New

World. Even today, in the so-called Age of Democracy, only a minority of states can truthfully be termed "democracies," as we see in later chapters. Still, given our basic thesis, how do we account for even this modest minority of democratic polities?

Many social scientists have sought to identify the conditions that make democracy sometimes viable, finding the answer in some special concatenation of social, economic, historical, and political factors (frequently referred to as "enabling" conditions). These factors, as we note in chapter 5, undoubtedly play a role and can help push humankind out of its default mode. Nonetheless, paradoxically enough, we must again turn to evolutionary theory for a better understanding of what makes democracy occasionally possible.

A neo-Darwinian approach holds that *Homo sapiens* shares the social primate proclivity for hierarchical social organization; but this approach also emphasizes that mankind has evolved some behavioral attributes and capacities that are, in effect, unique in the animal kingdom. There has been, of course, a long-running debate over whether other primate species are capable of language or, to take another controversy, of self-consciousness. Agreement on these matters has yet to be achieved. There is near-unanimity, though, that *Homo sapiens* alone has evolved the capability required to create, in more than very rudimentary form,[27] that vast complex of language, laws, customs and mores, art forms, material objects, technology, ideas, and values subsumed by the term "culture."

Robin Fox graphically describes the chasm between *Homo sapiens* and the other primates (1989: 28):

> Man is different from other primates, not because he has in some way *overcome* his primate nature, but because he is a different kind of primate with a different kind of nature . . . man behaves culturally, because mutation and natural selection have produced an animal that *must* behave culturally— invent rules, make myths, speak languages, and form men's clubs, in the same way as the hamadryas baboon must form harems, adopt infants, and bite his wives on the neck.

Some of the ideas and values that constitute so large a component of any people's culture are often attributed to a divine source; other ideas and values, especially those of a more secular character, have unmistakably human origins. Whatever their putative inspiration, these ideas and values, once brought into existence, are capable of profoundly altering the behaviors of those who believe in them.[28] This remarkable trait, manifested only by our own species, is what we have previously referred to as "indoctrinability."

When this occurs, humanity literally becomes the servant of its own creations;[29] in some instances, culture may even triumph, at least temporarily, over nature. True believers often willingly undertake actions and pursue goals that may be strikingly different from those to which our evolutionary history has otherwise predisposed us.

Religion offers the most familiar example of indoctrinability. Left to its own untutored impulses, mankind is all-too prone to engage, for example, in sex, aggression, and violence. Painfully cognizant of the enthusiastic readiness with which we pursue these activities, almost all religious codes strive earnestly to prohibit, or at least discourage, them.

Thus, almost all religions urge—or command—their followers to be chaste, if not celibate; not to be overly enamored of worldly possessions; to give to the poor; to forgive those who offend them; to be properly humble; even to love their neighbors as they love themselves. Granted, these commandments are not invariably obeyed. Nonetheless, religions have long demonstrated their ability to modify—sometimes drastically and sometimes only partially and transiently—the behaviors of their adherents. And, we might add, to evoke feelings of guilt—and thus possibly influence the future behavior—of those who transgress these teachings.

But religious beliefs are not the only source of behavior that literally runs against the biological grain. Secular doctrines no less than theological teachings have the same remarkable power. As repeatedly demonstrated over the centuries, social and political ideologies can also sometimes inspire their adherents to engage in actions, and to pursue objectives, which are at great variance from those to which their primate evolutionary legacy would otherwise incline them.

So, from time to time, and for reasons that differ from situation to situation, "democratic" ideas may gain acceptance among some sizable and/or influential segment of a nation's population. If this occurs in conjunction with some of the previously mentioned social, economic, and other, conditions, then and then only does a viable democracy become possible. Lamentably, it is not a conjunction that occurs very often.

This view of the matter suggests that perhaps another widely accepted idea should be turned on its head. The commonsense understanding is that the post–World War I triumphs of National Socialism and Fascism in Italy and Germany, and the subsequent post–World War II sweep of totalitarian Marxism in Eastern Europe and elsewhere, were to be explained in substantial part as the victory of clever totalitarian propaganda—that is, of effective indoctrination—over mankind's "natural" democratic preference. A contrary understanding may be closer to what actually occurred. By virtue of its genetic makeup, mankind may resonate much more readily to elitist and authoritarian ideologies. Accordingly, propaganda and indoctrination may account more plausibly for the occasional emergence of democracy than for the acceptance achieved by authoritarian beliefs and modes of rule.

To summarize—There is undoubtedly some validity to the notion that democracy demands certain "material" preconditions. But this familiar formulation overlooks the single most important requirement of all: for a democracy to be born and to survive also necessitates that nurture, in the sense of a compelling ideological conviction, triumph over nature, that is, our inherent primate predisposition for hierarchical social, and authoritarian political, systems. It is this second requirement, we suggest, that not only explains democracy's occasional appearance but also accounts for its infrequency, its frailty and, more often, its brief life span.

CHAPTER THREE
WHAT IS A DEMOCRACY?: TOWARD A WORKING DEFINITION

Introduction

This chapter presents the working, operational definition of democracy adopted throughout the remainder of this volume—a political system possessing competitive elections plus the protection of political liberties. However, to understand this perspective better, we need to have a sense of the range of views of what constitutes democracy.[1] In the following pages, we discuss several different contending orientations: democracy as process, participatory democracy, and democracy as polyarchy. Then, we briefly summarize three widely accepted databases upon which scholars draw in exploring the roots of democracy—because, in part, each of these identifies defining characteristics of democracy. The purpose of surveying the differing conceptualizations and operationalizations is simply to isolate defining characteristics of democracy by reviewing the larger literature.

Differing Views of Democracy

In this section, we summarize the key defining characteristics of democracy from three different philosophical perspectives. In the process, we find triangulation upon two central features of democracy. First, "democracy as process."

Democracy as Process: Schumpeter and His followers

Joseph Schumpeter is a well-known exemplar of this view. His starting point is what he calls the "classical doctrine of democracy," coming from the eighteenth century. He describes this doctrine as a set of institutional arrangements to make political decisions that lead to a realization of the common good, with the people deciding such issues through the election of officials empowered to implement the people's will. He describes one problem with this using a hypothetical situation (1975: 242).

> Let us transport ourselves into a hypothetical country that, in a democratic way, practices the persecution of Christians, the burning of witches, and the slaughtering of Jews. We should certainly not approve of these practices on the ground that they have been decided on according to the rules of democratic procedure. But the crucial question is: would we approve of the democratic constitution itself that produced such results in preference to a non-democratic one that would avoid them?

In short, the people can choose essentially evil or immoral goals.

Schumpeter prefers a process orientation toward understanding democracy. He is skeptical of the ability of the people as a whole to make good decisions. He has more faith in the capacity of elected representatives. Hence, he argues that (1975: 269) "the democratic method is that institutional arrangement for arriving at political decisions in which individuals acquire the power to decide by means of a competitive struggle for the people's vote." More simply, in the final analysis, "Democracy means only that the people have the opportunity of accepting or refusing the men who are to rule them" (1975: 285). Thus, democracy is conceived as a process, a political order in which the people turn effective power to decide over to those whom they elect.

Others have followed Schumpeter's lead. Popper notes that democracy is the only system by which people can rid themselves of their leaders without violence and bloodshed (Popper, 1962). Przeworski, too, asserts that the very possibility of government being turned out of office by voters renders conflict resolution more likely to be peaceful (Przeworski, 1999).

Here, the central defining characteristic of democracy is competitive elections, surely a hallmark of such a form of government. Of course, there are many critics of this minimalist perspective on democracy.[2]

Participatory Democracy

Peter Bachrach argues that the Schumpeterian view of democracy is really a hidden form of elitism, allowing real power to remain in the hands of a political directorate, with citizens having only the minimal role of voting for candidates to office. He contends that democracy can only remain a vital form of governance if there is widespread participation by the citizenry (Bachrach, 1967).

Bachrach's (1967: 101) central view is encapsulated in the following quotation:

> I believe that a theory of democracy should be based upon the following assumptions and principles: the majority of individuals stand to gain in self-esteem and growth toward a fuller affirmation of their personalities by participating more actively in meaningful community decisions; people

generally, therefore, have a twofold interest in politics—interest in end results and interest in the process of participation . . .

In addition, he contends that even private enterprises—if they have public effects—ought to be democratized, with people having a voice in decisions that have public effects.

Carole Pateman's *Participation and Democratic Theory* (1970) argues for the educative function of participation, following from John Stuart Mill's ideas; that is, people become more engaged and better citizens by the mere fact of participating. She also argues—as Bachrach—for citizens to be empowered to have decision-making roles in industry.

A final work on standard participatory democracy is the "Port Huron Statement," the founding document of the Students for a Democratic Society (SDS). At one point the document laments the lack of empowerment actually exercised by the American people (Students for a Democratic Society, 1985: 752):

> The very isolation of the individual—from power and ability to aspire— means the rise of a democracy without publics. With the great mass of people structurally remote and psychologically hesitant with respect to democratic institutions, those institutions themselves attenuate and become . . . progressively less accessible to those few who aspire to serious participation in social affairs.

The solution? To increase the ability of American citizens to participate effectively in the political realm. At one point, the document explicitly calls for participatory democracy (coursesa.matrix.msu.edu/~hst306/documents/huron.html):

> In a participatory democracy, the political life would be based on several root principles:
> - that decision-making of basic social consequence be carried on by public groupings;
> - that politics be seen positively, as the art of collectively creating an acceptable pattern of social relations;
> - that politics has the function of bringing people out of isolation and into community, thus being a necessary, though not sufficient, means of finding meaning in personal life . . .

In the final analysis, advocates of participatory democracy believe that the involvement of ordinary citizens in politics will empower them, will lead to their gaining confidence in the ability to participate meaningfully, will encourage them to become more informed about politics and policy issues, and will, in the process, enrich democracy.[3]

The central defining characteristic of this perspective is that there has to be openness in the political system to allow genuine involvement by the people. Thus, support for various forms of free expression and mobilization must be present for democracy to occur. Here, the key point is that civil liberties must be respected, to allow participatory democracy to flourish.[4]

Democracy as Polyarchy

One of the most influential strands of democratic theory comes from the work of political scientist Robert Dahl. From his *A Preface to Democratic Theory* (Dahl, 1956) to his *On Democracy* (Dahl, 1998), he has strenuously advocated the value of this form of democracy.

Dahl draws the term polyarchy from the Greek language, as opposed to monarchy (rule by one) or oligarchy (rule by a few). Polyarchy, on the other hand, stands for "rule by the many" (Dahl, 1998: 91). The original version of his formulation appeared in his 1956 work. Over time, the concept has been refined.

Dahl defines "rule by the many" in terms of six institutional characteristics:

1. Elected officials;
2. Free, fair, and frequent elections;
3. Freedom of expression;
4. Access to alternative sources of information;
5. Associational autonomy;
6. Inclusive citizenship.

A word about each is in order.

The criterion of elected officials refers to voters electing representatives to make decisions on their behalf. Thus, contemporary democracies in large countries are inherently defined as representative democracy. Elections must be freely contested and held relatively routinely.[5] Coercion in elections must be relatively rare for a country to be defined as democratic. Citizens must also have free expression, so that the incumbent regime can be criticized. To make informed choices at elections and to judge regimes in the interregnum between elections, citizens need to have access to a variety of information sources—not just sources controlled by the government.

Citizens need to be able to associate with one another during and between elections.[6] They must be free to join existing groups, to form new groups, and to take part in political contests. Participation in groups is a key mechanism for citizens to influence officials (e.g., see Dahl, 1960). Finally, inclusive citizenship. As Dahl (1998: 86) puts it, "No adult permanently residing in a country and subject to its laws can be denied the rights that are available to others and are necessary to the five political institutions just listed."

While Dahl is aware that this gives citizens less of a role than in participatory democracy (e.g., see Dahl, 1970), he contends that polyarchy is the most practical form of democracy in large, complex societies. For Dahl, then, two basic criteria are critical for defining democracy: meaningful elections and civil liberties and rights.

Studying Democracy: The Three Basic Data Sets

To explore the defining characteristics of democracy further, we examine three of the most widely used and respected data sets on democracy: Vanhanen's data set, the Polyarchy data set, and Freedom House ratings.

Vanhanen's Polyarchy Data Set

Tatu Vanhanen (2003) notes that his measure follows closely the logic of Dahl's Polyarchy model (not coincidentally, Vanhanen's website for the data is called the Polyarchy Data set).[7] The two variables that he uses to create his "Index of Democracy" are (1) percentage share of the vote cast in elections by minority parties/independent candidates; (2) percentage of the adult population that votes in elections. He sees the first as evidence of genuine competition and the second as an indication of free access to the ballot.

Vanhanen insists that for a country to be ranked as democratic it needs minority parties/independent candidates to receive at least 30 percent of the vote and it requires 20 percent turnout. He multiplies these together; if each threshold is reached and if the total score is six index points $(0.3 \times 0.2 \times 100)$, then a country is designated as a democracy.

The logic for the threshold values? Vanhanen (2003: 65) says, "If the share of the smaller parties is very low, for example, less than 30 percent of the votes cast . . ., the dominance of the largest party is so overpowering that it is doubtful whether such a country could be regarded as a democracy." He contends that anything lower than a 20 percent turnout suggests that prospective voters may not be fully free to vote, suggesting a problem with civil liberties.

Thus, Vanhanen recognizes two components of democracy: meaningful elections with genuine competition, and freedom of access to the ballot by individuals. For him, the latter stands as an example of protection of civil liberties and the rule of law, even though it is associated with elections.

Freedom House Ratings

Freedom House publishes a well-known annual report, *Freedom in the World*. This lists all countries on earth and then notes the extent to which each is—or is not—free. The Freedom House score is treated as a metric of democracy. Each year, a survey team[8] pores over a massive amount of information on each country and the members of the team rate each country on a series of items from 0 to 4, with 0 being the least free and 4 being the most free.

There are two dimensions to Freedom House scoring: (1) Political Rights and (2) Civil Liberties. For each dimension, there are a number of questions, each rated 0–4 as noted above. For Political Rights, there are a series of questions under the following categories—Electoral Process (e.g., "Is the head of state . . . elected through free and fair elections?" is one of three items under this heading); Political Pluralism and Participation (e.g., "Are the people's political choices free from domination by the military, [etc.]?"); Functioning of Government (e.g., "Is the government free from pervasive corruption?"); Additional Discretionary Political Rights Questions (e.g., "Is the government . . . deliberately changing the ethnic composition . . . to destroy a culture or tip the political balance in favor of another group?"). Points are then tallied. A score of 36–40 is coded as 1 (most free); 30–35 as 2; 24–29 as 3, and so on, until we get to the least free score of 7, which comes as a result of a country scoring only 0–5 points. A score of 1 stands for a free country in terms of political rights; 7 represents the least free rating a country can receive on this dimension.

The same process applies to the second dimension of Freedom House ratings—Civil Liberties. Specific categories here include Freedom of Expression and Belief (e.g., "Is there academic freedom . . . ?"); Associational and Organizational Rights (e.g., "Is there freedom of assembly . . . ?"); Rule of Law (e.g., "Is there an independent judiciary?"); Personal Autonomy and Individual Rights (e.g., "Is there equality of opportunity and the absence of economic exploitation?"). Scores of 0–4 points are accorded each specific item, as before, 53–60 points is counted as 1 (most free), with 0–7 points leading to a score of 7 (least free).

The two ratings are added together and then divided by two. Scores of 1–2.4 lead to a state being labeled "free"; 3–5.5 is "Partly free"; 5.5–7 is defined as "not free." For our purposes, the key thing to observe is that the two dimensions focus on elections and the political freedoms accorded to individuals.

Polity Ratings

The essence of the Polity ratings in terms of the conceptualization of democracy can be summarized as follows (Gurr et al., 1991 79):

> There are three essential, interdependent elements of democracy as it is conceived in the contemporary political culture of Western societies. One is the presence of institutions and procedures through which citizens can express

effective preferences about alternative policies and leaders. Second is the existence of institutionalized constraints on the exercise of power by the executive. Third is the guarantee of civil liberties to all citizens in their daily lives and in acts of political participation.

A series of specific measures is developed, and a coder rates each country on these concrete metrics. The categories being coded include the regulation of political participation (are certain groups advantaged or disadvantaged?); political competitiveness in elections; constraints on the chief executive; recruitment of the chief executive (How open is the process? Is the process characterized by violent seizure of power?); and complexity of authority structures (How centralized is government authority?).

Once each specific item is coded, a score for democracy is calculated (noting how collectively democratic the different dimensions are) and autocratic (how autocratic does a given country rank). The autocracy score is subtracted from the democracy score (the logic being that many societies have some characteristics of each—democracy and autocracy) and ten points are added to the ensuing total. The resulting score runs from 0 (least democratic) to 20 (most democratic).[9]

A Working Definition of Democracy

Introduction

We believe that the preceding discussion of different approaches to defining and measuring democracy show two distinct dimensions. Succinctly put, these are (1) government by the majority, and (2) what is usually called "the rule of law." We see that these two simple criteria are products of several different approaches to exploring democracy. One approach (Schumpeterian) emphasizes elections. Participatory democracy certainly reflects an awareness of the importance of elections and also demands that people have ample opportunities and the freedom to become involved in politics in many other ways than just voting. Polyarchy emphasized *both* elections *and* civil liberties. Thus, each of the theoretical perspectives examined speaks to one or the other or both of these characteristics.

This is consistent with one standard dictionary definition of democracy (Plano and Greenberg, 1993: 8–9):

> A system of government in which ultimate political authority is vested in the people. . . . Democracy may be direct, as practiced in ancient Athens and in New England town meetings, or indirect and representative. . . . Democracy requires a decision-making system based on majority rule, with minority rights protected.

A brief comment on each of these two defining aspects of democracy is in order.

"Majority Rule"

Practically everyone who has written on the subject includes, under this heading, a representative system of government, freely contested and meaningful elections, ultimate accountability of the representatives to the electorate, and equal weight of voting influence in the sense of wide, if not universal, suffrage embodying the principle, "one person, one vote."[10]

In a democratic system, the representatives are chosen by some type of popular vote, the specific method varying considerably from one country to another. To be truly democratic, the system must enable the majority—if there is a majority—to elect a roughly corresponding proportion of the representatives. Ideally, though not always invariably, the same provision would be made for some equitable method of minority representation. In all democracies, representatives are responsible to the electorate in that their constituents choose them and reelection is contingent upon the voters of that constituency.

Meaningful and openly contested elections demand some type of bi- or multiparty competition *and* the ability of all parties to put their case before the electorate to the best of the resources available to them. Elections may be openly contested, but if one party is so dominant that it need pay little attention to what the people desire, there is no meaningful alternative to which the voter can turn (Key, 1949).[11] Where a single party remains in office election after election, as has been the case in Latin America and elsewhere, there may be a legitimate question as to whether this criterion is being satisfied. Our own feeling is that "meaningful elections" should entail at least one major peaceful (i.e., electoral) turnover of office over, say, a 20-year span.

Majority rule also calls for a suffrage that gives the vote to most of the adult citizenry. Even those countries invariably recognized as democracies sometimes fall considerably short of *universal* suffrage because age, residence, literacy (and in one well-publicized instance, sex) qualifications may deny the ballot to some, or possibly a significant fraction, of the population.

"Rule of Law"

All of the aforementioned requirements, as well as a long list of civil rights and liberties, may be spelled out in a nation's constitution and laws. Nonetheless, as we have too often seen, these are of little value absent a judicial system capable of their effective enforcement. This package of factors, in essence, is what is meant by the term "the rule of law." Indeed, it is telling that Freedom House explicitly lists "Rule of Law" as one if its criteria for civil liberties.

Electoral rights and civil liberties need to be more than fine words on exquisite parchment. If those who lose an election are stripped of their civil rights, freedom, or property by a victorious majority, this is a dubious form of democracy. The rule of law requires an independent judiciary, a government willing to enforce even those judicial decisions it dislikes, and the effective protection of political and civil liberties against both public and private infringement. As Lord Acton (1877) remarked "The most certain test by which we judge whether a country is really free, is the amount of security enjoyed by minorities." The American institution of an independent judiciary still remains the basic model in this respect and may well constitute the single most important American contribution to democratic theory and practice.

Majority rule and the rule of law are thus the two indispensable components of democratic governance. The great irony, of course, is that while both are absolutely essential, they often conflict with each other and, as a result, have been a source of ongoing political controversy. But this fundamental contradiction cannot be escaped: It is the price of living in a democracy.

A concluding comment on majority rule and the rule of law. Admittedly, neither of these two requirements lends itself to very satisfactory quantification; in some instances, opinions about a given country will legitimately differ. Still, when we look at the several assessments and listings of democratic and nondemocratic governments cited below, there is far more agreement than disagreement. To paraphrase Justice Potter Stewart's famous comment about pornography, we may not be able precisely to define a democracy—but we usually know one when we see one.

Democracy and Nation Building

When we speak of "democratic nation building," we expect the end product—the new democratic government—to feature majority rule plus a rule of law that guarantees minority rights and political freedoms. If the emergent "democracy" does not meet these criteria, of course, we cannot accept that new state as a democracy. The next chapter outlines the nature of nation building, most often currently conceived of as democratic nation building. However, this discussion needs to be based on a conceptualization of the term "democratic." This has been the focus of this chapter.

CHAPTER FOUR
DEMOCRATIC NATION BUILDING: FROM CONCEPT TO OPERATIONAL "CHECKLIST"

Introduction

We begin this chapter by briefly reviewing the literature to develop a working definition of "democratic nation building." Second, we look at a series of case studies to identify the activities and commitments that countries engaged in nation building must make, and the conditions that should exist, if this enterprise is to be successful. Third, from that survey, we develop a "checklist" to be utilized by a country (say, the United States) in deciding whether or not to attempt nation building in a specific state (say, since one's reach should exceed one's grasp, Syria or Iran). Last, we take Germany and Haiti as cases in point and examine the extent to which the proposed checklist might have predicted the outcome of those nation building ventures.

In principle, we should begin by establishing a generally agreed upon definition of nation building and then narrow the application to *democratic* nation building. However, since the great bulk of the contemporary literature is concerned with the latter—that is, the deliberate attempt to establish a democratic regime in place of one that is not democratic—we will treat the two terms as synonymous and interchangeable.

Francis Fukuyama (2004a: 1), one of the relatively few people who have offered a specific definition, sees nation building as the process of helping to "create self-sustaining democratic political institutions and robust market-oriented economies . . ."[1] He then draws a very important distinction between "nation building" and "state building." The former actually refers to (2004a: 1) "creating or repairing all the cultural, social, and historical ties that bind people together as a nation." The latter, in contrast, aims at (2004a: 1) "creating or strengthening such government institutions as armies, police forces, judiciaries, central banks, tax-collection agencies, health and education systems, and the like."

Fukuyama argues that the process must proceed in two stages (see also Fukuyama, 2004b): first, the country must be stabilized with the provision of humanitarian assistance, rebuilding of infrastructure, disaster relief, and economic development. Only then, second, comes the building of self-sustaining political and economic institutions that can support competent democratic governance and economic growth. Thus, nation building involves stabilization of ties that bind a people together *as well as* supporting the construction of government institutions. Interestingly enough, Fukuyama does not define democracy (We addressed that task in chapter 3).

A RAND report goes into much more detail,[2] providing an operational definition of democratic nation building by looking at the commonalities in seven such interventions (Germany, Japan, Somalia, Haiti, Bosnia, Kosovo, and Afghanistan). The report seeks to establish those factors associated with success or failure. Among those linked to success were the use of force "to underpin a process of democratization" (Dobbins et al., 2003: 1), occupation, peace enforcement, stabilization, and reconstruction. Success is (2003: 2) "the ability to promote an enduring transfer of democratic institutions."

Roland Paris addresses an issue that initially seems far afield—*peacebuilding*. However, his analysis ends up very much on the mark for better understanding democratic nation building. For Paris, peacebuilding represents "postconflict missions . . ." with "the goal of preventing a recurrence of violence" (Paris, 2004: 2). What does this have to do with nation building? As he explains (2004: 5)

> Peacebuilding missions in the 1990s were guided by a generally unstated but widely accepted theory of conflict management: the notion that promoting "liberalization" in countries that had recently experienced civil war would help to create the conditions for a stable and lasting peace. In the political realm, liberalization means democratization, or the promotion of periodic and genuine elections, constitutional limitations on the exercise of government power, and respect for basic civil liberties . . .

On the economic side, liberalization refers, according to Paris, to the movement toward a market economy model. His study of 14 postconflict situations finds this liberal economic democracy model a common end goal of peacebuilders. In effect, what he terms peacebuilding looks very much like what others call democratic nation building.

Minxin Pei and Sara Kasper note three criteria that define nation building in its most general sense (2003: 2–3): (1) the goal of regime change or the survival of a regime that would otherwise collapse; (2) deployment and long-term commitment of a large number of ground troops to develop stability; (3) the use of the nation builder's military and civilian personnel to politically administer target countries. With regard to this last point, the authors contend that (2003: 2) "the United States exercises decisive influence in the selection of leaders to head the new regimes." To put their argument into the context of democratic nation building, the end result would not be just regime change or stabilization, but regime change toward democracy or stabilization of democratic regimes.

We must also keep in mind the admonition by Jennings (2003: 5) that "What has been missing [in democratic nation building] is not knowledge but perceived self-interest, political will, and an adequate attention span . . ." This suggests that we must realize that democratic nation building is not an easy and automatic process. "Shock and awe" do not automatically lead to democracy blooming in hitherto authoritarian countries.

For now, then, democratic nation building can be provisionally defined as the process by which outside countries endeavor to create democracy in formerly undemocratic societies or to maintain democracy in those countries currently democratic but, for some reason, under threat of losing democracy.

The Requirements for Successful Democratic Nation Building

The RAND report mentioned above suggests a number of prerequisites, including military presence over time by the occupying country, international police presence over time, reducing postconflict combat-related deaths, timing of elections, dealing with refugees and internally displaced persons, initial external assistance, external per capita assistance, external assistance as a meaningful percentage of GDP, and changes in per capita GDP. [3] This obviously entails a commitment to provide substantial resources to the redevelopment effort, to be willing to invest considerable time to nation building, to make sure that appropriate security arrangements are made. In short, the process cannot successfully be done quickly or "on the cheap."

Jennings, too, prescribes a detailed set of actions required for successful democratic nation building (2003: 6–7):

1. In the immediate aftermath of conflict, security and the rule of law must be created. This includes creation of indigenous security forces and the capability of arresting, detaining, and trying alleged offenders in fair ways.
2. The outside power must understand the political ramifications of any decisions made, must avoid arrogance, and cannot be seen as favoring one group over another (creation of "informal caste systems" in the words of the author).
3. Avoid behaving with suspicion toward all people in the target country; remove from authority those closely associated with the deposed regime.

4. Support the development of projects to restore infrastructure and help develop "social capital" in the target country.
5. Development of rules for understanding the relative roles of the military and civil authorities in the immediate period after the intervention by the outside power.
6. Develop advisory bodies from leaders in the target country not associated with the deposed regime, and slowly increase the country's governing authority.
7. Be willing to make a long-term commitment. Short-term and resource-poor efforts at nation building increase the odds of failure.[4]

Pei and Kasper assert that three key factors determine the likelihood of success. First, the target nation's internal characteristics are relevant. Profound ethnic disagreements, religious hostility, high levels of economic inequality, weak governing capacity of the target state, and lack of prior experience with constitutional governance work against a favorable outcome. Second, convergence of geopolitical interests. "Outside powers have a greater probability of success if their broad geopolitical interests dovetail with those of *both* the elites and the people in the target nation" (2003: 5). This is critical, since it provides a motivation for the outside party conducting the nation building efforts to persevere and invest into the operation. There also needs to be some degree of consensus about the new direction that the country is moving toward within the society of the target state.

Finally, success must be undergirded by a willingness of the outside power to invest substantial economic resources in nation building. As noted earlier, the process cannot be done "on the cheap." [5] The hoped for end result is that the financial investment triggers a self-sustaining economic development in the target country. Continually pouring money into a target state that cannot sustain its own economy is a losing proposition. One lesson from America's history at nation building, according to the authors, is that there have been times where there was no commitment to economic investment. For instance, the authors observe that (Pei and Kasper 2003: 6)

In Latin America, however, the United States typically failed to deliver substantial economic aid following its military interventions. To the contrary, in many instances, it took advantage of the target countries economically through sweetheart deals for American corporations.

Paris (2004) argues that the most promising strategy is IBL—Institutionalization Before Liberalization—that is, that peacebuilders should not immediately move toward economic and political liberalization.

Rather, they should first (re)build institutions so that there is a stable base.[6] Among the steps in this process are:

1. Wait until conditions are conducive for elections to take place.
2. Design electoral systems to reward moderate parties and candidates.
3. Work to develop a stable civil society.
4. Head off the emergence of "hate" speech.
5. Develop conflict-reducing economic policies.
6. In short, rebuild effective state institutions.

For Paris, there needs to be a two-step process: first, build institutions as a foundation; second, construct liberal structures on that foundation.[7]

Anthony Cordesman adds an additional and relevant point: nation building logistics and operations must be built into any planned intervention, if a successful after-war situation is to evolve.[8] He says that (2004: 48)

> The United States must never repeat its most serious mistakes in Iraq and Afghanistan. From the start, security and nation building must be a fundamental part of the planning and execution of military operations that are directed at foreign governments.

Toward an Operational "Checklist"

Based on the literature just surveyed, we have developed the following "checklist" to be used in assessing the prospects for successful nation building:

1. Willingness by the "outside" power(s) to invest resources, human and economic, in the target country.
2. Willingness to maintain a military and civilian presence over considerable time to secure order and enhance the odds of successful transition.
3. Commitment to reducing postconflict combat-related deaths.
4. Appreciation of the culture of the target country, and avoidance of arrogance, or seeming to denigrate the institutions and values of the people.
5. Work to restore infrastructure and human capital in the target country.
6. Remove from key positions in the target country those closely associated with the previous regime (if the transition involved replacing a regime, as opposed to supporting an already existing regime).
7. An understanding that deeply divided countries, whether on ethnic, religious, or economic lines, reduce the odds of successful intervention.
8. The interests of outside countries and internal constituencies in the target country must coincide—or must appear to coincide.

9. Rebuild social, political, and economic institutions as the base upon which liberal reforms can be constructed at a later time.

We will shortly apply this checklist to two case studies: Germany, after World War II, and the Haitian nation building undertaking in which the United States has been sporadically engaged for the past few decades, to see how it predicts the outcome of such ventures. Before we do that, however, it might be useful to look at three attempts to assess the results of nation building efforts over the past century.

The Record of Democratic Nation Building

The record makes it clear that democratic nation building is not an automatically successful process. Pei and Kasper (2003) enumerate the efforts of United States at nation building since 1900 (see table 4.1 for more detail). Of 16 occasions, 4 were successful (Germany and Japan after World War II, Grenada and Panama in the 1980s), and one is indeterminate (Afghanistan). All others were rated as unsuccessful, in that there was no functioning democracy ten years after the American intervention.

Dobbins et al. (2003) examine seven case studies—Germany, Japan, Somalia, Haiti, Bosnia, Kosovo, and Afghanistan. In their judgment, Japan and Germany were clear successes; Haiti, Somalia, and Afghanistan were failures. Kosovo and Bosnia are possible successes. What makes the difference between success and failure? The authors claim that (2003: 161) "what distinguishes these two groups is the levels of effort the international community has put into their democratic transformations." Successful nation building demands "time and resources" (2003: 161).

Paris's analysis of 14 case studies concludes that it is not easy to manage successful democratic nation building. While the majority of societies emerging from civil conflict do not revert to overt civil war (as has been the case with Angola, Rwanda, and Liberia), many others are still subject to low-grade internal conflicts (such as Mozambique, Cambodia, and Bosnia). One reason for this is (Paris, 2004: 6) "The very strategy that peacebuilders have employed to consolidate peace—political and economic liberalization—seems, paradoxically, to have increased the likelihood of renewed violence in several of these states."

Why would economic liberalization yield internal turmoil that threatens the ultimate effort to institutionalize liberal democracy? Because marketization is (Paris 2004: 235) "inherently tumultuous and conflict-promoting." And few of these "postconflict states" are able to handle such contentious situations. Although many international institutions seek to promote market economies, according to Paris (2004: 199), "The economic reforms

Table 4.1   U.S.-led nation building efforts since 1900

Target Country	Population	Period	Duration	Multilateral or unilateral	Type of interim administration	Democracy after ten years?
Afghanistan	26.8 million	2001–present	2+	Multilateral	UN	?
Haiti	7.0 million	1994–1996	2	Multilateral	Local	No
Panama	2.3 million	1989	<1	Unilateral	Local	Yes
Grenada	92,000	1983	<1	Unilateral	Local	Yes
Cambodia	7 million	1970–1973	3	Unilateral	U.S. surrogate regime	No
South Vietnam	19 million	1964–1973	9	Unilateral	U.S. surrogate regime	No
Dominican Republic	3.8 million	1965–1966	1	Unilateral	U.S. surrogate regime	No
Japan	72 million	1945–1952	7	Multi-unilateral[a]	U.S. direct administration	Yes
West Germany	46 million	1945–1949	4	Multilateral	Multilateral administration	Yes
Dominican Republic	895,000	1916–1924	8	Unilateral	U.S. direct administration	No
Cuba	2.8 million	1917–1922	5	Unilateral	U.S. surrogate regime	No
Haiti	2 million	1915–1934	19	Unilateral	U.S. surrogate regime	No
Nicaragua	620,000	1909–1933	18	Unilateral	U.S. surrogate regime	No
Cuba	2 million	1906–1909	3	Unilateral	U.S. direct administration	No
Panama	450,000	1903–1936	33	Unilateral	U.S. surrogate regime	No
Cuba	1.6 million	1898–1902	3	Unilateral	U.S. direct administration	No

Source: Pei and Kasper (2003).

[a] The United States won World War II as part of the Allied victory over Japan, but the United States assumed exclusive occupation authority in Japan after the war.

typically required by the IMF and World Bank tend not only to lower the living standards of certain groups within states undergoing adjustment but also to worsen the overall distribution of wealth in those states." In the final analysis, he contends that (2004: 205) "promoting democratization and marketization in institutionally weak, conflict-prone environments is an unreliable and potentially counterproductive approach to peacebuilding."

In sum, the studies summarized above conclude that democratic nation building is not an easy process, inevitably leading toward success.

Case Studies of Success—and Failure

To provide concrete illustrations of the process of democratic nation building, we examine briefly one case study in success, Germany, and another in failure, Haiti. These case studies provide more texture to the process than simply a survey of studies.

Germany

After World War II ended, Germany was a devastated country. The infrastructure was heavily damaged, the economy was in shambles. Large numbers of refugees lived in miserable circumstances. The key challenges immediately facing the Allies in the aftermath of war were restoring security, rebuilding civil administration, addressing the humanitarian crisis created by the war (some 21,000,000 persons were displaced in Europe), democratizing the defeated nation, and reconstructing the economy. One small plus for the Allies was that Germany had had some experience with democracy during the Weimar Republic.

How did the Allies meet these challenges? Very successfully. Germany has become viewed as one of the triumphs in democratic nation building in the twentieth century.[9] The first challenge was reestablishing security. Even with rapid American demobilization after World War II, four divisions remained in Germany; Great Britain, France, and the Soviet Union all had troops in the occupied country. American constabulary forces began to train German law enforcement personnel after the demobilization of the *Wehrmacht*, and within a few years, Germany (in the Allied zones) was able to maintain its own security.

The Allies, together with private agencies such as the International Red Cross, religious organizations, and the like, provided humanitarian assistance and help to refugees. The first step in establishing civil administration in the shattered country was to "denazify" German society. Many Nazi leaders were punished and excluded from leadership roles; the political and legal structures developed by the Nazis were dismantled. But not all former Nazis were purged. The Allies made use of mid-level bureaucrats to assist in reestablishing civil authority. Starting in 1949, Germany (outside of the Soviet sector) began to move toward sovereignty.

The American strategy to rebuild democracy in Germany was based on a "bottom up" perspective. Dobbins et al. emphasize that (2003: 15) "U.S. policy focused on a 'grass roots' approach, designed to build a German civil society from the bottom up." Political parties began organizing, first, at the county level and later, at the state (*Land*) level. The first countrywide election was held in 1949, with Konrad Adenauer elected as first chancellor of West Germany (i.e., the area administered by France, Great Britain, and the

United States). After the end of the war, the western sector also introduced basic civil liberties (freedom of speech, press, and assembly) and denazified the educational system.

The Nazi economic apparatus was terminated and the occupation forces became responsible for economic and budgetary policy. The German central bank continued to exist in the Western sector of Germany, but the occupying forces controlled its decisions. Industry began to revive. An important part of this overall picture was the Marshall Plan in 1949, which helped support rapid development of the German economy. Dobbins et al. conclude that (2003: 21)

> The most important lesson from the U.S. occupation of Germany is that military force and political capital can, at least on some circumstances, be successfully employed to underpin democratic and societal transformation. Furthermore, such a transformation can be enduring.

Haiti

Haiti's troubled history illustrates the difficulty of democratic nation building and democratic state building.[10] Haiti gained its independence in 1804, when a slave revolt ended French rule. Since then, the country has had a turbulent existence, with harsh poverty, a history of political violence, and dictatorships. We pick up our story in 1986, when the Duvaliers, who ruled Haiti for 29 years, were ousted from power.

After that, instability has been the order of the day. Under considerable international pressure, Haiti became a "democracy" in form in 1987, complete with a president, two legislative bodies, and a prime minister (appointed by the president). But it soon went from "partially free" to "not free," according to Freedom House ratings. President Jean-Bertrand Aristide, elected in 1990, was sacked by the military after several months in power. The brief rise to "partly free" status ended with that coup.

President Clinton led an intervention to "restore" democracy in 1994. American troops entered the country, and Aristide was restored to office. In the 1995 election, Aristide's candidate Rene Preval won the presidency handily, albeit with questionable election processes. Instability continued, however, and Aristide was reelected president in 2000. Unrest did not cease, and Aristide was deposed once more in 2004, at which time yet another United States-led international intervention took place to "restore democracy."

Let us take a look, briefly, at the details of the American effort to "restore democracy" in 1994.[11] Haiti is, by the way, a common case study used in analyses of democratic nation building—a classic instance of failure.

There was no substantial Haitian security force in place after the American intervention in 1994. There was only a weak governmental infrastructure; the economy was in terrible shape, with many people living in extreme poverty. Haiti ranks 150 out of 175 countries on the United Nations poverty list (Goldsborough, 2004a: A-14). The army was corrupt and ineffective, and provided no basis for indigenous security forces. In terms of government structure, before the intervention, Dobbins et al. write that (2003: 72–73)

> Aristide had been freely elected, but few other elements of a functioning democracy were available to be "restored." The Haitian parliament was corrupt and ineffective, the Haitian bureaucracy weak and incompetent, and the Haitian judiciary almost nonexistent.

The intervention consisted of American and other troops entering Haiti to restore order and return Aristide to power. The U.S. intervention was planned to avoid "mission creep" and become entangled too deeply in Haitian affairs, and it was designed to have a clear "exit strategy." These objectives, on their face, were achieved. Aristide returned; the military leadership was ousted; a new civilian police force was created; and routine violations of people's civil rights diminished greatly. However, the American government and the United Nations did not make a serious effort at economic reconstruction and building political institutions.

In the final analysis, as Dobbins et al. (2003: 74) summarize, "U.S. and other international forces departed, however, before a competent Haitian administration could be created, self-sustaining democratic structures could be put in place, or meaningful economic reforms could be instituted." A failure in democratic nation building.

Haiti is a classic illustration, then, of the difficulty encountered by a major power trying to impose democratic structures on a country with a long tradition of strong man rule, military dictatorships, and the like, without being willing to invest time, resources, and personnel. Then, in 2004, the United States and other countries once more intervened. Time alone will tell whether lessons have been learned from earlier failures in nation building in Haiti.[12]

There are those who still are optimistic about a better future for Haiti. Vicenzo (2004: G-6) argues that "There is hope for the Western Hemisphere's poorest nation if the international community remains engaged." He fears, however, that these hopes will be dashed, noting that (2004: G-6) "With troops in Iraq, Afghanistan and the global war on terrorism, the United States is unlikely to lead a Haiti operation beyond the immediate future or be directly engaged on other regional challenges." And, as Goldsborough (2004a: A-14) says, the 2004 intervention was basically "a repeat, on the cheap, of 1994, and we can expect the same result."[13]

In early 2005, the augury for democracy in Haiti is even less promising. Tropical Storm Jeanne wreaked havoc upon the country, and the government's inability to provide support (food and medicine) to the people has exacerbated the internal tensions. After the storm subsided, there have been some demonstrations in favor of returning former president Aristide to power, symbolizing the continuing political instability. It also makes the "democratic nation building" effort appear even less likely to culminate in a functioning democracy (Sontag and Polgreen, 2004).

Discussion

Table 4.2 serves to summarize results of the two case studies—Germany and Haiti. We apply the items on the checklist to these two examples of attempted democratic nation building. It is painfully clear that the Haitian experiment was doomed to fail. Only on one of the items does there appear to be compliance—booting Aristide out of the country was a half-way approach to replacing key figures in a previously failed regime. But that is it, as far as we can determine. On no other item on the checklist has there been any sustained progress.

Table 4.2   Checklist for successful democratic nation building

1. Willingness to invest resources, human and economic, in the target country by the outside power.	G
2. Willingness to be patient and to maintain a military and civilian presence over time to secure order and enhance the odds of successful transition.	G
3. Commitment to reducing postconflict combat-related deaths.	G
4. Appreciation of the culture of the target country, and avoidance of arrogance, seeming to denigrate the institutions and values of the people.	G
5. Work to restore infrastructure and human capital in the target country.	G
6. Remove from key positions in the target country those intimately associated with the previous regime (if the transition involved replacing a regime, as opposed to supporting an already existing regime).	G H
7. An understanding that deeply divided countries, whether on ethnic, religious, or economic lines, reduce the odds of successful intervention.	
8. The interests of outside countries and internal constituencies in the target country must coincide—or must appear to coincide.	G
9. Rebuild institutions as the base upon which liberal reforms can be constructed at a later time.	G

Notes: H = Haiti; G = Germany.

On the other hand, we see that considerable effort was expended on democratic nation building in Germany. Our best estimates indicate that the appropriate effort was made on eight of nine actions. It is hardly surprising, then, that the German effort was far more successful than the Haitian experiment.

Democratic nation building, the record testifies, is not an easy and automatic process. It calls for an investment of force, energy, money, and time in order to have a chance to succeed. The most obvious cause of failure is to "do it on the cheap," whether in terms of time or investment. However, it is also clear that, under certain conditions, the process can be successful. The "checklist" that we discussed earlier begins to identify what experience tells us is required if democratic nation building is to have a chance for success.

However, the juxtaposition of democracy and nation building (two separate concepts) mandates that we consider what factors might be critical for the establishment, nurturance, and continuation of democracy, a subject that we address in chapter 5.

CHAPTER FIVE

DEMOCRACY: THE REQUISITE "ENABLING CONDITIONS" — NO SMALL ORDER

As noted earlier, the term "nation building" originally referred to the process of establishing (or reestablishing) a political entity capable of governing a given population residing in a given geographic area (or areas) and recognized by other states as exercising sovereignty over that population and that territory. Accordingly, "nation building" could be used to describe the creation of any type of stable government. In present-day discourse, however, the term has become a euphemism connoting the process of creating a *democracy*, rather than of establishing a viable polity, democratic or not. The change, we think, is definitely for the worse, since the shift of meaning conceals the profound difference between the two tasks—*creating democracy is immeasurably more difficult than establishing other forms of government*.

Throughout human history, authoritarian governments of one type or another have been the rule and democracies, the striking exception. The former flourish in almost any setting; the latter, there is near universal agreement, require very special "enabling" conditions for their emergence and survival. Why this vast and consistent difference? Because, as earlier remarked, we (*Homo sapiens*) are social primates, disconcertingly akin to the chimpanzees, and several million years of evolution have endowed the social primates with an innate inclination to hierarchical social and political structures.

There are, in fact, two types of requirements with which we must be concerned in any nation building venture. The first, which relate primarily to conditions in the country where nation building is being contemplated, we will call *decisional requirements*. These are the conditions that should evaluated before making a "go, no go" decision and, unlike recent American practice, should be the basis on which this judgment turns. Do enough of these essential requirements for the development of democracy exist to warrant the adventure? If not, can we realistically expect to create them—and, if so, at what cost and over what time? Attempting to establish democracy in countries where these conditions are in short supply (or absent) can be a truly Sisyphean task.[1]

The second set of conditions that we will call *operational* relate primarily to the government making the attempt—that is, the United States. Do we have the knowledge and administrative skills required for nation building in this particular part of the world? Are we prepared to invest the necessary resources of money and manpower or are we counting on substantial assistance from other powers? And, no trivial matter, are we prepared for a long-term commitment or are we acting on the assumption that the transformation to a democracy will be a near-overnight accomplishment?

Both the decisional and operational requisite conditions are important; both, obviously, must be satisfied if nation building is to achieve its intended purpose. But it is equally obvious this careful and thoughtful assessment of the former will, in most instances, obviate the need to deal with the latter. Accordingly, this is where we will start.

Enabling Conditions: The "Decisional" Requisite Conditions

These conditions—which relate to the country chosen for nation building—are usually discussed, as we do below, under the familiar "social," "political," "economic," and other, headings. In real life, though, matters do not always fall out quite so neatly, since these categories often blur into one another. Consequently, there will no doubt be instances in which we place an enabling condition under one heading and the reader may justifiably feel that it could have been more properly considered under another. As one of our offspring is prone to say in such a situation, "whatever."

This is hardly the place to attempt a detailed discussion of any, let alone all, of the enabling conditions identified in the literature. This would constitute a substantial volume in itself. Our objective, rather, is to provide an operational "checklist" for those trying to decide whether or not a contemplated U.S. nation building enterprise in a given country has any realistic prospects of success. The choices made of late give little evidence that the presence or absence of these requirements has been taken into serious account, although techniques for actually measuring many of the items on the checklist have been developed to the point where, as we propose, the ultimate decision could be (and in Iraq and Afghanistan clearly should have been) based on some defensible "scoring" system.

Whatever the rank order of the other decisional considerations, one should go automatically and immediately to the head of the list. Not surprisingly, it is a viable state.

The Mother of All Conditions—*A Viable State*

If nation building means establishing a democracy, the indispensable prior objective must be a *state* capable of providing such basic, effectively functioning "governmental institutions and services as armies, police forces, judiciaries, central banks, tax collection agencies, health and education systems, and the like" (Fukuyama, 2004b: 159). State building (as in Afghanistan and much of Africa) or rebuilding (as was the case in Germany, Japan, and Iraq) thus must be the first goal. Until a "self-sustaining" government has been established, attempting to create a democracy is a guaranteed exercise in futility.[2] The newly established polity may not be notably democratic—but it will at least have the possibility of ultimately becoming so.

This raises, of course, the problem of attempting nation building in a country experiencing a civil war. To the degree that the rebels/insurgents/ freedom fighters, call them what you will, constitute a serious and ongoing persistent threat to the incumbent regime, there is a real question whether a "state," in the sense above, has yet been established. Conceivably, military intervention by a foreign power might end the conflict but intervention is not invariably successful; it may exact an increasingly burdensome cost on the intervening power; and the "indigenous" population may find it difficult to grasp the distinction between well-intentioned nation building and less laudable imperialist intentions, to mention only some of the possible negative consequences.[3] For much the same reasons, countries engaged in military conflict with their neighbors are dubious prospects for nation building. Maintaining civil rights and political freedom during a war is difficult enough, even in a well-established democracy; establishing and securing these de novo under wartime conditions has yet to be managed.

Economic Enabling Conditions

A per capita annual income of at least $5,000, Fareed Zakaria (2004) has recently written, is essential for a country to be a democracy.[4] One can quarrel with the amount but the underlying concept is sound: democracy is not likely to take root among a greatly impoverished people. Nor, as James Madison warned, is it likely to survive long in countries where there are great inequities of wealth between the masses and the few. Indeed, one of the most basic requisites for building a democracy is adequate economic development without vast disparities in wealth and income.[5]

Keeping in mind that the "have" nations are markedly outnumbered by the "have-nots," the present relationship between per capita income and democracy can be summarized as follows: With some exceptions (the Arab oil states, to be sure), the haves are more likely to be democracies; with few exceptions (India, at slightly less than $3,000), the "have-nots" are much more likely to have authoritarian or even totalitarian governments.

It would be strange if the relationship were otherwise. Impoverished nations almost always lack many, often most, of the other enabling conditions; they are also often racked by deeply divisive religious and ethnic differences, rendering near-impossible the mutual accommodations and compromises inherent in a democracy; and grinding poverty has denied the majority of anything beyond a rudimentary education, if that. Furthermore, there are the consequences of poverty itself—malnutrition,[6] wretched housing, high infant mortality, and, for those who survive, chronic ill health and a low average life span. Under such circumstances, getting food on the table today (if they have a table) may be more important than securing the right to vote tomorrow. Not surprisingly, a recent UN study found that half of those surveyed in Latin America "would prefer a dictatorship if that improved their living standards . . ." and that "democracy does not enjoy good health fundamentally because it has not provided benefits in terms of reduction of poverty and inequality" (Associated Press report cited by the *San Diego Union Tribune*, April 22, 2004, p. A-20).[7] Many Russians, looking back to what may now seem to be the "good old days," have expressed similar sentiments.

For these and other reasons, there is an inverse relationship between poverty and democracy—the poorer the people (as with the hapless Haitians), the bleaker the prospects for successful nation building (e.g., see Vanhanen, 2003). From a purely pragmatic perspective, the policy implications of this relationship speak for themselves. But pragmatism is one thing, and politics another. Barring a profound change in our approach to these matters, we can confidently look forward to further occasions when future American presidents, ala their predecessors, will again send in the Marines and proudly proclaim yet another restoration of democracy in Haiti—or some other equally unfortunate nation.[8]

Education

We are on solid ground in saying that democracy requires a reasonably well-educated citizenry—and that countries where the population is largely illiterate are hardly promising venues for nation building.[9] At the same time, we must be cautious in stating the relationship between the two. Peter Galbraith, for instance, has claimed that "education makes democracy possible, and along with economic development, makes it necessary, even inevitable" (1996: 72). The first clause is no doubt true—but the rest of the statement, even allowing for the elasticity of "inevitable," is hardly supported by the evidence. Only those with very short memories will find it difficult to think of several developed countries with a well-educated population—and unmistakably authoritarian governments.

Political Conditions

1. The Basic Liberties

As noted earlier, "freedom" and "democracy" are not synonymous terms. For the latter to be born, however, there must exist at least the basic rudiments of the former—freedom of speech, of the press, of assembly—and a judiciary able and willing to curb governmental transgressions of these liberties. Where these conditions are absent, they must be brought into existence—a task more often measured in decades than in years. On this score the former British colonies were relatively fortunate, since the British usually brought with them their respect for law and their tradition of judicial independence. Although the legacy was sometimes imperfectly transmitted and, after independence, too often sadly dissipated, in this respect the former British possessions are more promising candidates for nation building (actually, rebuilding) than those ruled by almost any other colonial power. Regrettably, none of these have been the countries to which the United States has directed its nation building talents.

2. Nature of Previous Regimes

A basic concern for liberty and due process, to repeat, is an important enabling condition. No less important, but more frequently encountered as a serious *liability* are the consequences of a previous authoritarian regime. As Gretchen Casper has succinctly remarked, "The legacies of authoritarian rule are fragile democracies" (1995: 5).

Casper studied nation building in the Philippines and several Latin American countries focusing on two major social institutions—the Roman Catholic Church and the military. Both institutions, she found, were profoundly changed by the experience of authoritarianism. In several instances, the Church and the army actually supported the attempts to overthrow an authoritarian regime. Nonetheless, she concluded, "When the country tries to return to democracy, these institutions cannot easily revert to their pre-authoritarian roles. . . . [and] try to remain in the political arena even after the democratization process has been introduced" (1995: 10). At best, their active participation in the political process produces uncertainty and instability; at worse, it contributes to the resurrection of authoritarianism, if in slightly different form.

Casper limited her study to nations in which the military and the Roman Catholic Church are politically important institutions and her findings have the greatest significance, therefore, for other countries where these two play similarly weighty roles. The logic of her analysis suggests, though, that other religious organizations (Moslem, Protestant, Greek Orthodox, Jewish, etc.) might be subject to the same pressures under authoritarian regimes and might behave in the same fashion if, when, and where democratization is attempted.

3. Presence of a Pro-Democratic "Out Elite"

Prospects for democratization are measurably improved if there already exist political figures (or even parties) who (that) have been openly critical of the previous regime and who are perceived by a sizable segment of the citizenry as favoring the creation of a more democratic polity. The absence of credible, potential democratic leaders, as was the case in Iraq and Afghanistan, makes even more difficult the task of establishing a government whose legitimacy will be broadly accepted.

Ironically, the presence of such an "out elite" can sometimes be almost as great a liability as it is an asset, once the previous regime has been overthrown. Too often and usually too late, we discover that some of the aforementioned "democrats" are primarily concerned with their own aggrandizement and with becoming an "in," rather than an "out" elite.[10] Nor have we always been adept, even with the invaluable guidance of the CIA, in distinguishing between those who really seek a more democratic society and those who employ the language of democracy primarily to further the political agenda of some religious, ethnic, or economic component of the population. Too often, as well, attempts to compromise disagreements among rival "pro-democracy" factions over how the new government should be structured result in "a useless piece of paper replete with noble axioms . . ." and a constitutional document, imposed from the outside, remarkably ill-suited both to the nation's immediate needs and to its level of political development (Ottaway, 2004: B-11). The history of American nation building provides ample examples of each, some, or even most of these problems.[11]

4. Pro-Democratic Civic Dispositions

For democracy to take root, especially in a newly liberated nation, a major proportion of the population and its political leadership must be willing to abide by three basic rules: to utilize discussion, persuasion, and voting as a means of resolving political issues; to compromise and settle for "half a loaf"; and to accept defeat peacefully, if not graciously, without resorting to arms. These habits come slowly and painfully.[12] Leo Strauss is often cited as the philosophical mentor for those who preach that it is our national mission to carry democracy abroad, one way or another. But, as one of his long-time

University of Chicago colleagues has cautioned, "Strauss would have seen as a historical distortion the idea that one could implant one's own culture on people who had not been taught it. . . . One could not liberate the citizens of a bad state and expect them to emerge from the war with a good state intact" (Karl, 2004: B-18). Or, as Stanley Hoffman has put it even more pointedly, "Democracy cannot be implanted surgically in countries that have no experience with it or preparation for it . . ." (2004: 7).

The act of liberation is therefore only the first, and in one sense, the easiest step in nation building.[13] Then begins the difficult task of inculcating what Jean Elshtain has aptly called the requisite democratic "dispositions":

> These include a preparedness to work with others different from oneself toward shared ends, a combination of strong convictions with a readiness to compromise in the recognition that one can't always get everything one wants, and a sense of individuality and a commitment to civic goods that are not the possession of one person or of one small group alone. (1995: 2)

Most critical of all, we should add, is an acceptance of, and a willingness to abide by, the basic tenets of democratic ideology. This acceptance, a relatively recent development in human history,[14] is not always readily forthcoming, because, like it or not, the egalitarian aspects of democratic theory run counter to our social primate inclinations. Furthermore, as we have so often seen, democratic values may also run counter to the loyalties and behaviors seemingly sanctioned, if not actually demanded, by competing belief systems (religion, nationalism, tribalism, etc.). John Milton's confident assurance notwithstanding,[15] the noblest ideas do not always triumph, even in "free and open encounter."

If we are not to blunder from one costly failure to another, we must put nation building in proper historical perspective. Democratic institutions, behaviors, and beliefs took centuries to develop in the United States and England. With these two as lodestones and guides, the subsequent transformation to democracy by several other Western countries in the late nineteenth and early twentieth centuries required, perhaps, a generation more. There is overwhelming evidence that "by themselves, the violent overthrow of a government and the initiation of radical change from above almost never fosters democracy, an expanded civil society, or greater openness" (Marshall, 2004: 112). The two most successful post–World War II nation building undertakings, Germany and Japan—countries that already had considerable experience with representative government—entailed several years of military occupation.

These realities stand in sobering contrast to the Alice-in-Wonderland schedules projected by our policy makers for the establishment of "peaceful, freedom-loving democracies" in Afghanistan and Iraq in particular and, even more preposterously, the entire Middle East.[16] The fate of 15 of the 16 countries constituting the former USSR poignantly demonstrates that although toppling a totalitarian regime is a necessary first step in nation building, it is very, very far from being a sufficient condition. But that is hardly surprising: Almost two decades ago, a young Russian academic warned that "Russia couldn't leap from totalitarianism to democracy but must transit through a long period of authoritarian rule." (Higgins, 2004: A-12).

Counter-Indicative Conditions

To this point, we have examined those conditions widely viewed as essential for successful nation building. Should many or most of these be present, the prospects for a viable democracy, given adequate time, are relatively favorable—that is, keeping in mind our innate tendency toward hierarchy and the consequent historical predominance of authoritarian regimes. If many or most of these conditions are not present, well, this is a matter to which we return shortly.

Now for the other side of the coin. As we have so often seen the past few decades, there are "five deadly enemies of democracy" (deep-seated religious, national, ethnic, racial, and tribal differences)[17] whose presence, individually or in consort, not only almost always preclude nation building but also make it nearly impossible to establish any government not perceived as grossly unfair and discriminatory by many of its citizens. Conceptually, to be sure, the five are distinct;[18] in real life, however, they often overlap and reinforce each other, sometimes to the point where the disputants deny the humanity of their opponents. One of the most perverse consequences of these differences "is the 'racialization' of culture—the tendency to think of another people as not just culturally but genetically distinct"—and to act accordingly (Olson, 2002: 227). As alleged (all-too often, correctly) offenses are repaid with compound interest, over the decades there develops, for each side, "a history of grievous wrongs committed by the other" (Schwartz, 2004: 110). There are always atrocities to be avenged and a score to be evened. Before long, understandings of, and preferred solutions to, today's issues are shaped and colored by perceptions of innumerable past injustices and horrendous misdeeds. All too soon, this mental set takes on a near-impenetrable life of its own. As a sage once remarked, "Others fear what the morrow may bring, but I am afraid of what happened yesterday" (Tuchman, 1981: 268).[19]

1. Religious Differences

Of the five, religious differences are probably the most virulent, possibly because they so often go hand-in-hand with at least one of the others.[20]

A few examples should suffice: Religious rivalries still pose a serious threat to democracy in India and to date have been an insuperable barrier to a unified, democratic Ireland. The situation is much bleaker in Central Europe, some of the African nations, and in East Asia where massacres, genocide, and ethnic cleansing have become accepted methods of settling religious (and ethnic, racial, and tribal) conflicts thereby leading to depths of politically sanctioned human behavior that come perilously close to rivaling those of the Holocaust itself.[21] In almost all of these countries, any attempt to resolve religious differences, as Bernard Lewis sadly remarked, swiftly takes the form—"I'm right, you're wrong, go to Hell" (2003: 36–42).

Although all four of the major religions (Christianity, Hinduism, Judaism, and Islam) have been involved in one or more of these conflicts, the opposition to nation building efforts in Afghanistan and Iraq has led some writers to suggest that Islam, by its very nature, is inherently authoritarian (Manji, 2004),[22] a contention given *prima facie* support by the fact that of the 56 officially Muslim states in 2003, not one was a democracy (*The Economist*, November 15, 2003: 10).[23] That contention was met by the argument that, since "it took over 200 years for the United States to reach its present state of perfection . . . we might at least give Iraq and the other Arab states a generation or two (Gelb, 2004: A-12).[24] Perhaps a more middle-of-the-road and persuasive explanation for the failure of Western-type democracy to take root in the Middle East "is that Arab nationalists have wanted to pick and choose from the Western cornucopia, taking over science and technology and/or educational systems and/or institutions of government without being ready to absorb their philosophical underpinnings as well, the false gods of rationalism, skepticism, and materialism" (Coetzee, 2003: 4).

2. Nationalism, Ethnicity, Race, and Tribalism

Together with religion, these are surely today's most divisive issues, far more so than such political ideologies as communism, fascism, or even democracy. As with religion, bitter differences in any of these areas are almost always fatal to the prospects of nation building and, in many instances, even to the chances of stable government.[25] Africa is especially vulnerable in this latter regard: "[S]ince most Africans feel more loyal to their tribe than to the young and artificial nation-states of which they are nominally citizens, it is often easy for unscrupulous leaders to win support by appealing to bigotry" (*The Economist*, January 17, 2004: 10). In all fairness, though, appeals to ethnicity and race by demagogues in other parts of the world have been just as effective in setting people against one another as tribalism has been in Africa, and the end results—violence, mayhem, rape, murder, ethnic cleansing, and genocide—just as appalling.[26] Ironically, some of the worst of these conflicts have been "between peoples who are physically indistinguishable— Palestinians and Israelis, Serbs and Albanians, Irish Catholics and Irish Protestants, Muslims and Hindus from India, Dayaks and Madurese from Indonesia" (Wilson, 2002: 226).

Once upon a time, in a more civilized era, national, ethnic, racial, tribal (and religious) adversaries might reasonably ask, "Why should we be a minority in your state when you can be a minority in our state"?[27] Today, in one country after another, this question seems to have become "Why should you exist at all, at least in our state"? "Modern human invaders," in the judgment of one observer, "have compiled an almost unbelievable abominable archive in their behavior toward resident human populations, let alone other species" (Tattersall, 2002: 136). Perhaps Barrington Moore was not altogether mistaken when he voiced the suspicion that "one of the few lasting and dependable sources of human satisfaction is making other people suffer (1964: 338). As Pascal remarked several centuries ago, "Men never do evil so completely as when they do it from religious conviction."

Fairness requires that we at least mention that some social scientists have argued that religious belief is a necessary prerequisite for democracy. Summarizing the pros and cons of the resulting debate, Arnold Brecht (1959: 458) spoke of the substantial evidence: thus "[F]irst, that democracy is in need of a consistent injection of ethical impulses, and second, that these impulses—within the framework of the typically democratic institutions and attitudes—were supplied in the past, and are still being supplied, chiefly by religious feelings." Clearly, the religious fanaticism with which we have become all too familiar the past few decades falls far outside the boundaries of Brecht's "typically democratic" attitudes.

Applying the Checklist: Democracy in Iraq and Afghanistan?

We earlier suggested the possibility of a "feasibility checklist" that might be used in the decisional process. Each of the "conditions" discussed above could be rated on, say, a four- or five-point scale ranging from "totally absent" to "fully adequate" (or equivalent terms). Depending on the nature of the condition (whether requisite or counter-indicative), the rating would translate into a numerical positive or negative value, adding or subtracting from the total score. This score, in turn, would be a quantitative indicator of the degree to which a given country is a likely prospect for nation building—just as high school grades and SAT scores are used in college admissions as predictors of an individual's academic potential.

Rather than simply discuss the possible merits of such an approach, we decided to put it to an actual test. Toward this end, we selected two U.S. attempts at nation building—one (Germany) clearly successful, one (Haiti) clearly not so (see the discussion of these two case studies in chapter 4). To what extent, if at all, would the proposed rating system have predicted the eventual outcome? For this "thought experiment," we decided on a simple two-step scoring system—either a given requisite was present or not,[28] and gave equal weight to each item on the checklist.

Our first step was to develop a checklist (table 5.1) for the "decisional" requisites. If the letter "G" appears on a line, this indicates that the condition was met for Germany after World War II; an "H" indicates that Haiti met that condition in the 1990s. As table 5.1 clearly shows, Germany satisfied many more decisional conditions than Haiti—eight for the former, only two for the latter. To be sure, there could be some question about crediting Germany with the "existence of civil liberties" (Item 5). This, however, has been basically the case both for the First Reich and in the Weimar Republic. In any event, table 5.1 leaves little doubt that nation building in Haiti, insofar as there was any expectation of short-term results, was doomed to failure.

The difference in prospects between the two countries is even more striking when we consider the "operational" checklist for democratic nation building (See table 5.2), already presented with a fuller discussion, of course, in chapter 4. Germany meets most conditions, Haiti only one. Given this disparity, it was hardly surprising that one was a success and the other, well, something less than that.

All in all, then, this modest experiment suggests that the literature on the prerequisites for democratic nation building has accurately identified the conditions associated with success or failure in that undertaking. But these are retrospective tests applied after the fact. Would they be equally useful if utilized in situations where the outcome still hangs in the balance? The next step, then, was to apply the proposed rating system to our two most recent forays into nation building. Table 5.3 gives the results of ratings involving the "decisional" prerequisites in Iraq and Afghanistan. The results are hardly encouraging.

Table 5.1   Checklist for emergence of a democracy

1. Functioning government institutions	G
2. Internal peace (e.g., no civil wars)	G
3. Adequate levels of economic development	G
4. Adequate levels of education	G
5. Existence of basic liberties	G
6. Lack of previous authoritarian regime	
7. Pro-democratic "out-elite"	G
8. Pro-democratic civic dispositions	
9. Religious conflict is absent	G H
10. Ethnic, tribal, and racial conflict is absent	G H

Note: H = Haiti; G = Germany.

Iraq has two of the preconditions potentially conducive to democracy—adequate levels of economic development and adequate levels of education. Afghanistan? Here, the prognosis seems even bleaker; only one of the prerequisites is met—relatively little religious conflict in this largely Islamic country.

Table 5.4 examines the "operational" conditions for successful democratic nation building in Afghanistan and in Iraq after overwhelming military

Table 5.2 Checklist for successful democratic nation building

1. Willingness to invest resources, human and economic, in the target country by the outside power.	G
2. Willingness to be patient and to maintain a military and civilian presence over time to secure order and enhance the odds of successful transition.	G
3. Commitment to reducing postconflict combat-related deaths.	G
4. Appreciation of the culture of the target country, and avoidance of arrogance, seeming to denigrate the institutions and values of the people.	G
5. Work to restore infrastructure and human capital in the target country.	G
6. Remove from key positions in the target country those intimately associated with the previous regime (if the transition involved replacing a regime, as opposed to supporting an already existing regime).	G H
7. An understanding that deeply divided countries, whether on ethnic, religious, or economic lines, reduce the odds of successful intervention.	
8. The interests of outside countries and internal constituencies in the target country must coincide—or must appear to coincide.	G
9. Rebuild institutions as the base upon which liberal reforms can be constructed at a later time.	G

Note: H = Haiti; G = Germany.

Table 5.3 Checklist for emergence of a democracy

1. Functioning government institutions	——
2. Internal peace (e.g., no civil wars)	——
3. Adequate levels of economic development	I
4. Adequate levels of education	I
5. Existence of basic liberties	——
6. Lack of previous authoritarian regime	——
7. Pro-democratic "out elite"	——
8. Pro-democratic civic dispositions	——
9. Religious conflict is absent	A
10. Ethnic, tribal, and racial conflict is absent	——

Note: I = Iraq; A = Afghanistan.

victory had been achieved, the two former regimes overthrown, and the process of transforming these two countries into "peace loving democracies" formally launched.

Table 5.4 makes rather uncomfortable reading. For whatever reasons, the United States has been a good deal less generous to Afghanistan than to Iraq. At the most recent count, the United States has invested some $200 billion in the latter; our major benefaction to Afghanistan, at least to date, appears to be the Kabul–Kandahar road. Although the United States has made some efforts to rebuild and restore essential infrastructure in Iraq, much less has been done in Afghanistan.

Beyond this, the United States has been fairly even-handed. We have visited death and destruction on both countries; some estimates have it that 100,000 Iraqis have been killed since the brief war terminated, although the actual number may more likely be between 15,000 and 18,000 civilians ("Iraq Body Count," 2005). In both, incumbents from the previous regime were removed from office; in both, the United States has made some effort to recognize the difference between their cultures and ours; in both, we have underestimated the power of tribal and ethnic differences; in both, we are desperately searching for an "exit strategy"—hardly in keeping with

Table 5.4 Checklist for successful democratic nation building

1. Willingness to invest resources, human and economic, in the target country by the outside power.	I
2. Willingness to be patient and to maintain a military and civilian presence over time to secure order and enhance the odds of successful transition.	___
3. Commitment to reducing postconflict combat-related deaths.	___
4. Appreciation of the culture of the target country, and avoidance of arrogance, seeming to denigrate the institutions and values of the people.	I A
5. Work to restore infrastructure and human capital in the target country.	I
6. Remove from key positions in the target country those intimately associated with the previous regime (if the transition involved replacing a regime, as opposed to supporting an already existing regime).	I A
7. An understanding that deeply divided countries, whether on ethnic, religious, or economic lines, reduce the odds of successful intervention.	___
8. The interests of outside countries and internal constituencies in the target country must coincide—or must appear to coincide.	___
9. Rebuild institutions as the base upon which liberal reforms can be constructed at a later time.	___

Note: I = Iraq; A = Afghanistan.

the operational requirement of patience, patience, patience. And in both, the burning desire for this strategy has worked against the process of gradually building (or rebuilding) social and political institutions supportive of democratic governance (a point well made by Fukuyama).

The scores in tables 5.3 and 5.4 tell the tale all too clearly. On the decisional prerequisites (table 5.3), Iraq meets three out of ten conditions, Afghanistan one in ten. Neither approaches Germany's eight but both are disconcertingly close to Haiti's two. Table 5.4, which deals with the operational requirements, is only slightly less discouraging, with Iraq satisfying four, and Afghanistan two, of the nine conditions for successful nation building. On the same scale (table 5.2), the reader may recall, Germany scored a nine and Haiti a dismal one. Taking these scores at face value, the prospects for a democratic Iraq are less than encouraging—though considerably brighter than for Afghanistan.

There is, to be sure, the objection that, given the "requisite conditions" we have identified, very few countries will emerge as promising candidates for nation building; that we have, in effect, "stacked the deck"; and that, if the United States were to adopt this approach, we would only rarely pursue that objective. To which we can only reply—yes, no, and yes.

Yes—very few countries have the conditions needed for successful nation building, as the term is now understood. No—we did not stack the deck. These are the conditions that almost everyone who has studied the matter agrees are essential for a viable democracy. Their absence is not of our making but, in the final analysis, a consequence of human nature in general and of *Homo politicus* in particular. As for abjuring nation building, yes, indeed. This is precisely the point of this book—nation building, as we practice it,[29] has been demonstrably an almost hopeless undertaking, best abandoned, and the resources turned instead to strengthening and preserving democracy here at home.

CHAPTER SIX
WILL THE REAL DEMOCRACIES PLEASE STAND UP?

Introduction

To be a democracy, then, a government must have, *de minimus*, two characteristics—majority rule and the rule of law. Applying this rather generous definition, we can now test our contentions that (1) nation building, with very, very few exceptions, has been a failed enterprise, and that (2) democracies, even in a vaunted eponymous age, remain very much a minority among governments.[1] But first, a brief word about the history of democracy.

A Brief History of Democracy: Early Intimations

A well-known early example of democracy is Athenian democracy. This was not the type of democracy familiar to Americans. Athens emphasized participation within the democracy as educational, instilling a sense of citizenship and civic virtue in the people. It was a form of direct democracy, with the citizens themselves making basic legislative and judicial decisions (e.g., see Ober, 1993). Athens was hardly an ideal democracy: slavery rests uneasily with democracy; women were not allowed to participate; those who were eligible to participate were a small minority of all; majority tyranny was an omnipresent danger (as witness the circumstances surrounding the death of Socrates). Nonetheless, for the time in which it took place, Athenian democracy was remarkable.

Next came the Roman Republic, which provided another democratic exemplar for later ages, although, as with Athens, the existence of slavery cannot be ignored. Under the Republic, and probably until the Emperors were accepted as near-deities, the will of the majority and the actions of governmental officials were seen as properly constrained by Roman law.

Possibly because of this, Roman democracy was the longer-lived of the two, although Athens' defeat by Sparta almost certainly hastened, if it did not actually cause, the demise of popular rule. In any event, majority governance in Athens lasted considerably less than a century by the most generous reckoning. The much longer-lived Roman democracy, on the other hand, was destroyed from within.[2]

However, there were many flaws with these early harbingers of democracy, such as class differences, slavery, many citizens not being represented at all, and a poorly articulated ideology supportive of widespread, broad-based democratic institutions.

Contemporary Democracy

A decade ago we conducted a census of democracies,[3] and we reported the following:

1. Needless to say, the United States was the first modern democracy, attaining that status ca. 1830–1850. By the end of the nineteenth century, a half-dozen other countries (including, at one time or another, Canada, France, Switzerland, Belgium, and New Zealand) could also be so categorized (Vanhanen, 1990). Over the following decades, the number grew both slowly and erratically depending primarily on the political circumstances but also on the criteria employed by those doing the classification.[4]
2. As of 1995 there were 199 so-called sovereign states. Of these, however, 41 were "microstates" with a population of less than one million. This left 148 "macrostates" in our set of countries to be studied.
3. Of the 148, only 28 (i.e., 19 percent) could reasonably be called democracies, using our two touchstones. This 19 percent figure coincided almost exactly, we should note, with Freedom House's 1996 rating of "free nations"—19.6 percent.

Ten years have passed we reported this census. Where does democracy stand today in the family of nations? Given our focus on nation building, are there new democracies and, if so, how did they come into being? Has the number—or percentage—of democracies in the family of nations changed and, if so, in what way? And, most central to this book, does our census yield very persuasive evidence of successful democratic nation building?

Counting Democracies in the Early Twenty-First Century

The first step—deciding which nations fall under our purview—is relatively simple. We use the listing of countries in three studies—Polity, Vanhanen, and Freedom House.[5] Each has essentially the same enumeration of countries year-to-year. We deleted all microstates (i.e., those states with less than one million population) from consideration, leaving a data set composed entirely of macrostates. So far so good.

While the years covered by these ratings do not precisely track year-by-year, there are numerous points in time at which we have data from all three studies. Of course, there are some lingering issues. These studies do not define democracy in precisely the same manner; they use different methodologies and scoring systems.[6]

This left us with the task of converting their different scoring systems (Freedom House employs a tri-partite "free," "partly free," and "not free"; Polity gives a grade rating for extent of autocracy and extent of democracy [one subtracts the autocracy score from the democracy score to get a sense of how democratic a state is]; and Vanhanen uses two electoral measures).[7] Although the terms are not exactly synonymous, we treated the Freedom House ranking of "free" as the operational equivalent of "Democratic"; countries receiving either of their other two designations were classified as "Not Democratic."[8]

We adopted an analogous solution in converting the Polity ratings. We counted as democracies all of those countries with a score of 8 or more. Finally, those countries designated by Vanhanen as democracies were also counted by us.

This is probably the appropriate place to comment on the hazards and possible pitfalls of these rankings and the danger of awarding the encomium of "democracy" too easily and too soon. A 2002 UN study reported that only 82 out of 140 countries that have had held "democratic" elections since 1980 could also claim a free press and an independent judiciary (United Nations Development Programme, 2002). Nor were "democratic" constitutions a reliable indicator. As the study director remarked, "We are seeing a rise of the situation where the constitution is barely respected, especially in Latin America." Further worsening the situation was the tendency for the military to intervene in civil affairs in the Far East and in sub-Sahara Africa. Endorsing the study's conclusions, Catherine Dalpino, a Brookings Institution fellow, criticized "the international community [for] forcing democracy in a hothouse atmosphere . . . [you] can't manipulate a country into democracy. You can manipulate a country into an election" (in Donnelly, 2003; see Dalpino, 1998, 2000).

In addition to the reservations expressed in the UN report, the decision as to whether a given country is or is not a democracy (or is "free") has other problematic aspects. Western social scientists, by and large favoring that mode of government and desirous of seeing it more widely adopted, may sometimes be tempted to employ this designation on the basis of less persuasive evidence than the circumstances actually warrant. A typical instance was a "streamer" on the cover page of the usually reserved *Economist* (as well as a glowing story) entitled "Indonesia's shining Muslim democracy," based largely on the successful completion of an election in 2004.[9] No doubt, this was a truly encouraging development for a country rated as "partly free" in the most recent Freedom House survey. Nonetheless, everything considered, it was perhaps a bit premature. In marked contrast, the newspaper summary of the UN report mentioned above was captioned, with depressing accuracy, "New democracies face long, hard slog." Students of animal behavior are always cautioned against the so-called anthropomorphic bias; Western—and especially American—social scientists who look for signs of democracy may occasionally manifest an analogous tendency.

Time, in a very literal sense, is also a potentially distorting factor. Examining a large number of nations and, in the many instances where the decision is by no means self-evident, gathering and assessing the requisite information takes considerable time. Organizing the material, writing up the results, editing, and actual publishing can easily take many months, sometimes even longer. Consequently, the published findings, no matter how sound, can only mirror the situation a year or more earlier—but much could have happened, especially in young and/or unstable countries, to drastically alter the political situation during that interval.[10] These published data are akin to light from a far distant celestial object: they tell us what the situation was some time in the past—but not necessarily what it is today. In part for that reason we have occasionally questioned some of the Freedom House and/or Polity ratings.

Finally, we should not forget that, however encouraging these assessments of democracy and freedom may seem to be, we still "live in a world in which, at least for three-quarters of the human population, the idea of human rights is no more than rhetoric, and not a reality in everyday life" (Cavalieri and Singer, 1993: 5). This bleak reminder is probably as true today as it was a decade ago.

So much for caveats, cautions, and disclaimers. Now to the data.

The Data: Step I—Counting Democracies

First, what have been the trends in democracy over time? At the beginning of this chapter, we summarized Vanhanen's analysis. However, for another view, we consider Robert Dahl's work. Dahl, using longitudinal data displayed in table 6.1, plots the number of democracies versus the number of nation-states *in toto* (Dahl, 1998). One thing to note with Dahl's data is the exemplification of Samuel Huntington's thesis of the "three waves" of democracy (Huntington, 1991, 1991–1992). From Dahl's table, one observes a rise in democracy into the 1930s; however, there is a reduction in numbers by 1940. The rise beginning after World War II is interrupted by a decline in 1980. Since, there has been upward movement in democracy. However, the lesson of history should be heeded: retrograde movement may follow upward movement in democratization.[11]

Table 6.1 Democratic countries as a percentage of all countries

Date	Number of countries	Number of democracies	Percentage of democracies (%)
1860	37	1	3
1870	39	2	5
1880	41	3	7
1890	42	4	11
1900	43	6	14
1910	48	4	16
1920	51	15	34
1930	64	22	34
1940	65	19	29
1950	75	25	33
1960	87	36	41
1970	119	40	34
1980	121	37	31
1990	192	65	34

Source: Robert A. Dahl (1998).

Next, using the methodology noted in previous pages, we use three separate sources to assess the current roster of democracies (for another approach, see Somit and Peterson, 1997): Vanhanen, Polity, and Freedom House—for 2001. Thus, we have data from three different respected sources for one year. These approaches to measuring democracy have already been described in the third chapter. Table 6.2 provides a listing of countries that are deemed democratic by at least two of the three sources. We use this table to address two issues: (1) the extent to which democracy is ascendant throughout the world; (2) more important to the thrust of this volume, the extent to which democratic nation building has contributed to the increase in the number of democracies, as portrayed by both Dahl and Vanhanen in their time series examination.

We label each country as democratic (using the terminology of Vanhanen and the Polity study) or free (the Freedom House term that stands as a surrogate for the label of democracy).[12] If all three identify a country as democratic, we note that in the column named "Ranking." If two of the three sources term a country as free or democratic, we rate the country "Near D" (near democratic) in that column.

One could surely argue that this is a generous assessment. The Human Development Report 2002 raises some very real questions about how democratic some of these nations actually are (United Nations Development Programme, 2002; and see Schedler, 2001). However, this serves as a starting point. Table 6.3 summarizes the percentage of democracies and near democracies.

Table 6.2 Comparing three ratings of democracy, 2001: counting those countries with two or three indices indicating democratic status

Country	Vanhanen	Polity	Freedom House	Ranking
Argentina	D	D	PF	Near D
Australia	D	D	F	D
Austria	D	D	F	D
Belgium	D	D	F	D
Benin	D	Near D	F	Near D
Bolivia	D	D	F	D
Botswana	D	D	F	D
Brazil	D	D	F	D
Bulgaria	D	D	F	D
Canada	D	D	F	D
Chile	D	D	F	D
Costa Rica	D	D	F	D
Croatia	D	D	F	D
Czech Republic	D	D	F	D
Denmark	D	D	F	D
Dominican Republic	D	D	F	D
Estonia	D	Near D	F	Near D
Finland	D	D	F	D
France	D	D	F	D
Germany	D	D	F	D
Ghana	D	Near D	F	Near D
Greece	D	D	F	D
Hungary	D	D	F	D
India	D	D	F	D
Ireland	D	D	F	D
Israel	D	D	F	D
Italy	D	D	F	D
Jamaica	D	D	F	D
Japan	D	D	F	D
Korea, South	D	D	F	D
Latvia	D	D	F	D
Lithuania	D	D	F	D
Macedonia	D	D	PF	Near D
Malaysia	D	D	PF	Near D
Mexico	D	D	F	D
Mongolia	D	D	F	D
Netherlands	D	D	F	D
New Zealand	D	D	F	D
Nicaragua	D	D	PF	Near D
Norway	D	D	F	D
Panama	D	D	F	D
Papua New Guinea	D	D	F	D
Peru	D	D	F	D
Philippines	D	D	F	D

Continued

Table 6.2 Continued

Country	Vanhanen	Polity	Freedom House	Ranking
Poland	D	D	F	D
Portugal	D	D	F	D
Romania	D	D	F	D
Senegal	D	D	PF	Near D
Slovak Republic	D	D	F	D
Slovenia	D	D	F	D
South Africa	D	D	F	D
Spain	D	D	F	D
Sweden	D	D	F	D
Switzerland	D	D	F	D
Taiwan	D	D	F	D
Thailand	D	D	F	D
Trinidad and Tobago	D	D	PF	Near D
United Kingdom	D	D	F	D
United States	D	D	F	D
Uruguay	D	D	F	D

Note: For the Polity score, 8 or higher is considered to be democratic; 6–7 is coded as near democratic.

Table 6.3 Percentage of countries that are democratic or near democratic

No of countries	No of democracies	% of Total	No of near democracies	% of total
149	51	34	9	6

Of 149 macrostates (we do not count states whose population is less than 1,000,000 persons, using population data appearing in Vanhanen, 2003), 51 (34 percent of the total) can be deemed full democracies. Nine other countries (6 percent of the total) are what we call "near democracies" with two of three measures indicating the existence of a democracy. Even adding these together, 40 percent of the world's countries can be judged democratic. This is hardly a majority, and, as noted, one can be skeptical that all of these countries are actually democratic.

However, the preceding data are rather static. Even Dahl's time series design gives only an aggregate look at changes in the amount of democracy throughout the world. We do know that some countries move from undemocratic to democratic status, and others switch from being democratic to becoming undemocratic. We need to capture this dynamic element in order to get a fuller picture of the process of democratization. As we shall see in the following paragraphs, the data make it clear that much movement takes place over decade-long intervals. This suggests some degree of instability in the status of states. It also suggests that even if there is a successful venture in democratic nation building, one cannot be assured that a country attaining democratic status will automatically retain it.

To assess the dynamics of democracy, we used Freedom House data at four points in time: 1973, 1983, 1993, and 2003. Table 6.4 summarizes the dynamics of democratization from 1973 through 2003.

A number of readings of these data provide useful information about the nature and process of democratization over the past 30 years.

First, by Freedom House definition, of 126 states, 33 were democratic in 1973 (26 percent), 38 of 140 were so judged in 1983 (27 percent), 42 of 148 in 1993 (36 percent), and 61 of 148 in 2003 (41 percent). This indicates stability in democratization between 1973 and 1983, acceleration

Table 6.4 Freedom House: ratings over time: 1973–2003

Country[a]	1973	1983	1993	2003
Afghanistan	PF	NF	NF	NF
Albania	NF	NF	PF	PF
Algeria	NF	NF	NF	NF
Angola	—	NF	NF	NF
Argentina	PF	PF	F	F
Armenia	—	—	PF	PF
Australia	F	F	F	F
Austria	F	F	F	F
Azerbaijan	—	—	PF	NF
Bahamas	—	F	F	F
Bangladesh	PF	PF	F	PF
Belarus	—	—	PF	NF
Belgium	F	F	F	F
Benin	NF	NF	F	F
Bolivia	PF	F	F	PF
Bosnia-Herzegovina	—	—	NF	PF
Botswana	PF	F	F	F
Brazil	PF	PF	F	F
Bulgaria	NF	NF	F	F
Burkina Faso	PF	NF	PF	PF
Burma	NF	NF	NF	NF
Cambodia	NF	NF	NF	NF
Cameroon	PF	NF	NF	NF
Canada	F	F	F	F
Central African Republic	NF	NF	PF	NF
Chad	NF	NF	NF	NF
Chile	F	NF	F	F
China	NF	NF	NF	NF

Continued

Table 6.4   Continued

Country[a]	1973	1983	1993	2003
Colombia	F	F	PF	PF
Congo (Brazzaville)	NF	NF	PF	PF
Congo (Kinshasa)	NF	NF	NF	NF
Costa Rica	F	F	F	F
Cote d'Ivoire	NF	PF	PF	NF
Croatia	—	—	PF	F
Cuba	NF	NF	NF	NF
Czechoslovakia	NF	NF	F	—
Czech Republic	—	—	F	F
Denmark	F	F	F	F
Dominican Republic	F	F	F	F
Ecuador	PF	F	F	PF
Egypt	NF	PF	PF	NF
El Salvador	F	PF	PF	F
Eritrea	—	—	—	NF
Estonia	—	—	PF	F
Ethiopia	NF	NF	PF	PF
Finland	F	F	F	F
France	F	F	F	F
Gabon	NF	NF	PF	PF
Gambia	F	PF	F	PF
Georgia	—	—	PF	PF
Germany, E	NF	NF	—	—
Germany, W	F	F	—	—
Germany	—	—	F	F
Ghana	NF	NF	PF	F
Greece	NF	F	F	F
Guatemala	F	NF	PF	PF
Guinea	NF	NF	PF	F
Guinea-Bissau	—	NF	PF	PF
Haiti	NF	NF	NF	NF
Honduras	PF	F	F	PF
Hungary	NF	NF	F	F
India	F	F	PF	F
Indonesia	PF	PF	PF	PF
Iran	NF	NF	NF	NF
Iraq	NF	NF	NF	NF
Ireland	F	F	F	F
Israel	F	F	F	F
Italy	F	F	F	F
Jamaica	F	F	F	F
Japan	F	F	F	F
Jordan	NF	NF	PF	PF
Kazakhstan	—	—	PF	NF
Kenya	PF	PF	PF	PF
Korea, N	NF	NF	NF	NF
Korea, S	NF	PF	F	F

Continued

Table 6.4 Continued

Country[a]	1973	1983	1993	2003
Kuwait	PF	PF	PF	PF
Kyrgyz Republic	—	—	PF	NF
Laos	PF	NF	NF	NF
Latvia	—	—	PF	F
Lebanon	F	PF	PF	NF
Lesotho	NF	PF	PF	F
Liberia	NF	NF	NF	NF
Libya	NF	NF	NF	NF
Lithuania	—	—	F	F
Macedonia	—	—	PF	PF
Madagascar	PF	PF	PF	PF
Malawi	NF	NF	NF	PF
Malaysia	F	PF	PF	PF
Mali	NF	NF	F	F
Mauritania	NF	NF	NF	NF
Mauritius	F	F	F	F
Mexico	PF	PF	PF	F
Moldova	—	—	PF	PF
Mongolia	NF	NF	F	F
Morocco	PF	PF	PF	PF
Mozambique	—	NF	PF	PF
Namibia	—	—	F	F
Nepal	NF	PF	F	PF
Netherlands	F	F	F	F
New Zealand	F	F	F	F
Nicaragua	PF	PF	PF	PF
Niger	NF	NF	PF	PF
Nigeria	PF	F	PF	PF
Norway	F	F	F	F
Oman	NF	NF	PF	NF
Pakistan	PF	NF	PF	NF
Panama	NF	PF	PF	F
Papua New Guinea	—	F	F	PF
Paraguay	PF	PF	PF	PF
Peru	NF	F	PF	F
Philippines	PF	PF	PF	F
Poland	NF	NF	F	F
Portugal	NF	F	F	F
Romania	NF	NF	PF	F
Russia	—	—	PF	PF
Rwanda	NF	NF	NF	NF
Saudi Arabia	NF	NF	NF	NF
Senegal	NF	PF	PF	F
Serbia-Montenegro	—	—	—	F
Sierra Leone	PF	PF	NF	PF
Singapore	PF	PF	PF	PF
Slovakia	—	—	—	F
Slovenia	—	—	F	F
Somalia	NF	NF	NF	NF

Continued

Table 6.4 Continued

Country[a]	1973	1983	1993	2003
South Africa	PF	PF	PF	F
Spain	NF	F	F	F
Sri Lanka	F	F	PF	PF
Sudan	NF	PF	NF	NF
Swaziland	PF	PF	PF	NF
Sweden	F	F	F	F
Switzerland	F	F	F	F
Syria	NF	NF	NF	NF
Taiwan	NF	PF	PF	F
Tajikistan	—	—	NF	NF
Tanzania	NF	NF	PF	PF
Thailand	NF	PF	PF	F
Togo	NF	NF	NF	NF
Tunisia	NF	PF	PF	NF
Turkey	PF	PF	PF	PF
Turkmenistan	—	—	NF	NF
Uganda	NF	PF	NF	PF
Ukraine	—	—	PF	PF
Union of Soviet SR	NF	NF	—	—
United Arab Emirates	NF	PF	PF	NF
United Kingdom	F	F	F	F
United States	F	F	F	F
Uruguay	PF	PF	F	F
Uzbekistan	—	—	NF	NF
Venezuela	F	F	PF	PF
Vietnam, N	NF	—	—	—
Vietnam, S	PF	—	—	—
Vietnam	—	NF	NF	NF
Yemen, N	PF	NF	—	—
Yemen, S	NF	NF	—	—
Yemen	—	—	PF	PF
Yugoslavia	NF	NF	PF	—
Zambia	PF	PF	F	PF
Zimbabwe	NF	PF	PF	NF

[a] Countries over 1,000,000 in population.

from 1983 to 1993 (an increase of percentage of democracies by 9 percent), and a smaller increase to 2003 (5 percent).

Second, what about new countries rated during the latter three time periods (i.e., countries that became recognized as states during the decade preceding one of the four columns in the table)? In 1983, three new countries were rated as "not free" (Guinea-Bissau, Mozambique, and Vietnam), whereas two new states were listed as "free" (Bahamas and Papua-New Guinea). In 1993, four new states were "not free" (three from the old Soviet Union and one from the disintegrating Balkans—Bosnia-Herzegovina), fourteen were "part free" (nine of which were from the old Soviet Union and four from countries that had been behind the iron curtain), and five were "free" (Czech Republic, Germany, Lithuania, Namibia, and Slovenia). There were rather few new states in that of 2003. Of the three new states emerging between the 1993 rating and that of 2003, one was "not free" (Eritrea) and two were free (Slovakia and Serbia-Montenegro).

Another approach that we have taken to explore the dynamics of democratization over the past three decades was to count the movement from democratic to nondemocratic status among states as well as the opposite movement—from nondemocratic to democratic. Table 6.5 summarizes the decade by decade movement in states' status.

From 1973 to 1983, we counted the number of macrostates that moved in a more democratic direction (i.e., from not free to partly free or free or from partly free to free). We did the same thing from 1983 to 1993 and from 1993 to 2003. We also counted those states moving in the contrary direction, from more free to less free, over that same period. From 1973 to 1983, eight states moved from less free to more free. From 1983 to 1993, this number jumped sharply to twenty-six states marching toward greater freedom. Finally, from 1993 to 2003, twenty-one states became more free.

What of the converse? From 1973 to 1983, twelve states became less free. This means that, net, four more states moved from more free to less free. From 1983–1993, we see evidence of some degree of acceleration in democratic emergence. Only eleven states moved from more to less free, meaning that there was a net movement in the direction of greater democracy by eleven states. And, most interesting, from 1993 to 2003, the number of states becoming less free was exactly the same as the number becoming more free—twenty-one—for a net change of zero in terms of movement toward or away from democracy.

One way of putting this is that the momentum toward democracy from 1983 to 1993 appears to dissipate by 2003, with movement toward and away from democracy equal in the subsequent decade.

One final approach is to look at the broad sweep of change from 1973 to 2003. One hundred seventeen countries serve as our database, the set of countries remaining the same from 1973 to 2003 (e.g., North and South

Table 6.5 Movement in democracy versus nondemocracy

Type of movement	1973–1983	1983–1993	1993–2003	Total change over time
Less free to more free	8	26	21	
More free to less free	12	11	21	
Net change	−4 (Less free)	+11 (More free)	0 (No change)	+7 (+11−4)

Table 6.6 Category to category change, Freedom House ratings, 1973–2003

Movement from 1973–2003	N
Not Free to Not Free	27
Not Free to Part Free	10
Not Free to Free	19
Part Free to Not Free	5
Part Free to Part Free	17
Part Free to Free	7
Free to Not Free	1
Free to Part Free	6
Free to Free	25

Vietnam disappeared in the 1970s and only Vietnam remained; it would not be counted in this table). Table 6.6 summarizes.

First, it is clear that some "not free" and some "free" countries were quite stable. Twenty-seven countries "not free" in 1973 were still "not free" in 2003. Twenty-five countries were "free" in 1973 and remained "free" in 2003. Second, we see that twenty-nine countries went from less free to more free from 1973 to 2003—while only twelve countries went from more free to less free over the 30-year period.[13] This surely testifies to an overall increase in freedom in the world. Finally, seventeen states were "part free" in 1973 and remained so in 2003.

The Data: Step II—Nation Building Success

Now, let us revisit table 6.2 to examine the success of democratic nation building. Of that roster, only two clear-cut cases of successful democratic nation building emerge: Japan and Germany. This, then, seems to recapitulate the findings from chapter 4, on nation building. And both these countries are the products of democratic nation building efforts that are a half-century old. Some might claim that, for instance, the Dominican Republic emerged as a democracy shortly after the intervention of Lyndon Johnson in the middle-1960s. However, Pei and Kasper (2003) label that effort a failure. Some suggest that Panama is a successful case too. Indeed, Panama is now rated as democratic by our methodology. However, we must await the test of time before confidently stating that this is a stable democracy. Thus, of 60 states that can generously be considered as the universe of democracies in 2001, only two would appear to be unambiguous examples of successful nation building.

A final test regarding nation building looks to the residue of the breakup of the Soviet Union. At the time of the breakup of the "Evil Empire," many spoke of the potential of increasing democracy emerging from the rubble of the old Soviet Union.[14] Table 6.7 provides an assessment of how free each constituent part (a former S.S.R., or "Soviet Socialist Republic") was as of 2001–2002, using Freedom House figures.

The Freedom House score for the Soviet Union was 5 (for political freedoms) and 4 (for civil freedoms) for 1990–1991, rendering it "part free." The column headed 2001–2002 in table 6.7 notes the current Freedom House status in that year. Outside of the three Baltic states of Estonia, Latvia, and Lithuania, there are no unalloyed democracies. At best, there are some Part Free countries (Armenia, Azerbaijan, Georgia, Moldova, Russia, and Ukraine). The rest are not Free (including Belarus, Kazakhstan, Kyrghyz Republic, Tajikistan, Turkmenistan, and Uzbekistan). More poignantly, the Freedom House score for the Soviet Union in 1990–1991, just before the empire's disintegration, was 5,4. Including the three Baltic states, the average 2001–2002 score is 4,4 (still "part free"). However, without those three states, the average would be 5,5, marginally worse off in terms of democracy, when compared with 1990–1991.

Thus, democracy has not yet bloomed in the old Soviet Union. Given that the international community has provided loans and other support to Russia and constituent countries of the old empire, efforts to strengthen the economies and nurture more liberal political structures have not yet succeeded. Hence, there is little indication that democratic nation building has taken root in the ruins of the Soviet empire.

Table 6.7   Status of the countries of the former USSR

Country	1990–1991	2001–2002
U.S.S.R	5,4 Part Free	
Armenia		4,4 Part Free
Azerbaijan		6,5 Part Free
Belarus		6,6 Not Free
Estonia		1,2 Free
Georgia		4,4 Part Free
Kazakhstan		6,5 Not Free
Kyrgyz Republic		6,5 Not Free
Latvia		1,2 Free
Lithuania		1,1 Free
Moldova		2,4 Part Free
Russia		5,5 Part Free
Tajikistan		6,6 Not Free
Turkmenistan		7,7 Not Free
Ukraine		4,4 Part Free
Uzbekistan		7,6 Not Free

Note: Summary score (including Baltic states) = 4,4 "part free"; Summary score (excluding Baltic states) = 5,5 "part free."

Discussion

So, what do the data tell us? First, democracy remains a minority among the world's nations. By our metric, 34 percent of the states on earth can be labeled as democratic. A small percentage of additional states can be termed near democracies. Surely, there is good news in this, since these numbers are greater than in the past. Nonetheless, it is clear that a majority of governments are still not democratic.

More to the point, given the aim of this book, what has been the success of democratic nation building over time? The results of our analysis are not encouraging. Few apparent successes have emerged. When democracies emerge, it appears that this phenomenon is more likely to be the product of the enabling factors that we have already spoken about rather than a result of conscious efforts by nations intervening to create democracies where, before, there were none.

CHAPTER SEVEN

AMERICAN NATION BUILDING, 1945–2005: COSTS AND CONSEQUENCES

To summarize our argument so far: With rare exceptions, attempts to export democracy (i.e., nation building) have failed. They have failed because (1) as social primates, our species has an inherent bias toward hierarchical political and social systems; (2) given this innate bias, democracy requires special "enabling conditions"; and (3) these conditions cannot be created overnight but take literally decades to evolve and mature. In support of this admittedly neo-Darwinian explanation, we noted the overwhelming predominance of authoritarian polities throughout history; that even today democracies still constitute only a modest minority of the world's governments; and that nation building has so far achieved very few successes.

But this is plainly a double-edged explanation. The same social primate hierarchical tendencies that require special conditions to make democracy possible also demand the perpetuation of those conditions if the democracy is to survive. And that, of course, is the great danger. Of all polities, democracies are the most fragile. Weaken or destroy the conditions that make them possible and they collapse. In contrast, when authoritarian regimes are overthrown, with few exceptions they are replaced by some other version of "rule by the few"—historically the "default" mode of governance.

Such is the situation, we fear, increasingly faced by the United States. In pursuit of our efforts to extend the blessings of democracy to less-fortunate— if sometimes vexingly unappreciative—peoples, we are hastening the erosion of the conditions on which our own democracy rests. To be sure, nation building did not set this erosion into motion—but in many problem areas it has significantly accelerated the process; in others, it has consumed the resources that could have been used to slow or even correct it. Just as George Kennan lamented in opposing U.S. involvement in Vietnam, our nation building forays into Afghanistan and Iraq, "[have] proceeded at the cost of the successful development of our life here in this country. It has distracted us and hampered us in our effort to come to grips with domestic problems of such gravity as to cry out, as we all know, for the concentrated, first-priority attention of both our government and our public" (Stael, 2004: 8).

But the damage has not simply been to democracy here in America. We are only being modestly chauvinistic in saying that our wealth, military power, and the freedoms of which we are so proud, have made us the avatar of democracy in the eyes of the world. Nation building—or, more precisely, the manner in which we have recently conducted it—has both lessened our standing in the eyes of the international community and, in many countries, adversely affected popular attitudes toward democracy itself.

With few exceptions, nation building has been demonstrably unsuccessful. But it has been worse than a failure. The most tangible results of our post–World War II attempts to export democracy have been to aggravate problems at home and, in all probability, diminish its prospects abroad. This, in essence, is the central theme of this chapter and a further basis for our gravamen against this policy.

How has nation building adversely affected our country? The question can be best answered, we think, if we look at the two distinct periods or phases (we will use the terms interchangeably) of American nation building policy over the past 60 years. The first, the so-called Cold War phase, ran approximately from the mid-1940s to the collapse of the Soviet Union; the second, imaginatively termed the post–Cold War phase, dates from this point to the present. The two phases differ considerably in their dynamics and in their objectives; those differences notwithstanding, the two had essentially the same destructive consequences at home and abroad. The similarity of these consequences demonstrated once again that those who will not learn from history are doomed to repeat it.[1]

Nation Building, Phase 1

Driven by the fear of Communist expansionism, primarily as exemplified by the USSR,[2] American foreign policy during the Cold War sought two objectives: first, in Kennan's classic formulation, "containment"; second, as reflected in the Marshall Plan, to preserve democratic government where it already existed and to encourage it where it did not.[3] But, it soon became apparent that the two were not of the same importance: the first was far more equal than the second. When forced to choose between supporting an admittedly authoritarian but presumably anti-Communist regime (or party), on the one hand, and a professedly more democratic but possibly more "Leftish" regime (or party) on the other, American diplomacy commonly gave democratic considerations short shrift. Our operational maxim, especially in Latin America but elsewhere as well, was unmistakably "anti-Communism uber alles." Inevitably, other nations soon realized that a mere hint of being receptive to Soviet blandishments could be remarkably effective in securing U.S. foreign aid.[4] As retired Marine General Tony Zinni recalled, "During the Cold War, no one ever let a little remote country in the middle of nowhere go wobbly, because every little country was involved in the competition between the Soviets and the Free World. Each side invested what it took to keep the little countries in their camp. Though these investments went by names like 'foreign aid' and 'humanitarian assistance,' they were actually payoffs" (Clancy, 2004: 176). As a result, we supported a number of undeniably repressive regimes, something their citizens may have forgiven but perhaps not forgotten.

What did Cold War nation building achieve? Beyond doubt, it played a major role, as previously discussed, in establishing or reestablishing democratic governments in West Germany and Japan. What, then, were the negative consequences? To begin, there was the cost in dollars and cents. Between 1947 and 1990, the United States spent a bit more than a *trillion* dollars on "international development and humanitarian assistance" and "international security assistance." [5] This trillion dollars could have gone a long, long way (the purchasing power of the dollar over this period was at least double its value today) to alleviate the grave social and economic problems that were already troubling this nation—and to which we will shortly return.

The actual monetary cost, though, was only one aspect of the matter. Characteristically confident of succeeding where the French had so dismally failed, nation building zeal drew us into Vietnam and, step by step, into what become the Vietnam War. The political furies and bitterness engendered by this war, the pros and cons of which were still being angrily argued in a presidential campaign several decades later, distracted the nation from giving our domestic problems the attention they badly needed. Over the intervening decades, few of them have disappeared or lessened; many have worsened and become even less tractable.

There was one other unhappy consequence for which we are still paying a price. The Vietnam War, and especially the manner in which it was conducted,[6] evoked in the "Woodstock generation" (and in many of its elders) a profound distrust of politics, politicians, and of the American democratic political system itself, a sentiment soon reinforced by the Watergate revelations of the early 1970s. Ironically, this distrust lent credibility to the conservative insistence during the 1980s that the less government, the better off the nation would be, and to President Reagan's mantra that government was not the solution but, rather, the problem.[7]

By the mid-1960s, foreign perceptions of our nation building efforts were influenced less and less by grateful memories of generous American post–World War II aid (gratitude having a famously short half-life) and increasingly colored by the Vietnam War. Viewed from abroad, we were fighting an unnecessary war, for the wrong reasons, with the wrong ally, in the wrong place and, given our reliance on air power, with a callous unconcern as to whether we were killing combatants or luckless civilians. Understandably, there were few nations where anti-American sentiment did not find repeated popular expression, just as did the antiwar feelings here at home.

Last, and no doubt worst of all, we lost the war. Much is forgiven the victor, very little the loser. The eventual peace treaty left us less respected, less feared, and certainly less admired than when we began. To the very real degree that the status and prospects of democracy are closely linked to that of the United States,[8] both suffered serious diminution.

Nation Building, Phase 2

Beginning with the collapse of the Soviet Union and the end of the Cold War, this phase encompasses the closing years of President George H. W. Bush's administration, the two terms of President Clinton, and the first term of George W. Bush. What objective(s) did American nation builders pursue during this approximately 15-year span?

The speeches of President Clinton and of the senior Bush reflected the widely accepted belief that "as both a moral and practical matter, promoting democracy around the world is in the long-term interest of the U.S. . . . ." (Dionne, 1991: 351). Nonetheless, establishing a democratic Iraq was certainly not an objective of the first Gulf War. President George H. W. Bush voiced no such intention and his abrupt termination of the conflict, leaving Saddam Hussein securely in power, deliberately put an end to this possibility. Although President Clinton often expressed his support of nation building, his administration was not notably more aggressive or successful than its predecessors in furthering this cause, although American troops were dispatched to places such as Kosovo[9] and Haiti presumably for this purpose.

President George W. Bush repeatedly spoke of his opposition to nation building during the 2000 presidential campaign.[10] Sometime after the election, however, he seems to have experienced a change of heart.[11] Although the invasion of Afghanistan in 2002 was initially justified on the grounds that the Afghan government had refused to turn over the Osama bin Laden terrorists responsible for "9/11," this *causus belli* was subsequently expanded to include the intent—nay, the moral duty—to democratize Afghanistan, a sentiment at least then perhaps not widely shared by the Afghani people themselves.

Iraq represents an essentially similar shift of justification. The initial rationale, as advanced by Secretary of State Powell in his speech before the United Nations, was that Saddam Hussein had accumulated vast stores of "weapons of mass destruction" (WMDs). Despite the American emphasis on the danger posed by Hussein's putative WMDs, there is considerable evidence that the "democratization" of Iraq had been contemplated, if not actually decided upon, very early in the Bush administration (Suskind, 2004). In any event, this objective soon joined the WMD threat as compelling reasons for inflicting "shock and awe" on the Iraqis.[12]

In Afghanistan, then, the Taliban's refusal to assist in rounding up the 9/11 culprits and in Iraq the dangers posed by the WMDs were the primary justifications given, respectively, for launching an invasion. In both instances, however, the desire to bring "democracy and freedom" to the Afghanis and the Iraqis were soon adduced in further support of this action. In neither case was nation building initially identified as the major American goal; in both cases it seems to have been moved to front and center[13] only after formal military hostilities had been triumphantly concluded and the postwar occupation begun. However belatedly the United States achieved this salience, President Bush's commitment to nation building was resoundingly reaffirmed in his Second Inaugural Address. It would be the policy of his administration, he assured—or perhaps warned—his audience, "to seek and support the growth of democratic institutions in every nation and culture, with the ultimate goal of ending tyranny in our world."

So much for the rationale. What was accomplished—and at what cost?

Afghanistan and Iraq: The Fruits of Nation Building

The Costs to Afghanistan and Iraq

Although our major concern in this chapter is the cost of nation building to the United States, we can hardly ignore the price paid by the Afghanis and the Iraqis. Regrettably, we can do this only in very sketchy fashion. As yet, neither of these two countries has a government able to provide much information on the subject; the previous American occupation officialdom had other more urgent matters requiring its attention; and, given their focus on terrorist and insurgent activities, it has not been a topic that has received more than casual coverage from our media. Understandably, it is a subject on which our own government has little incentive to be overly candid—and own media, if foreign critics are to be taken seriously, have been less informative than might have been the case.[14]

Iraq

Thanks to television, we have a pretty good idea of the destruction wreaked on many Iraqi cities, first by the war and then by the postwar disorders. We get some sense of the damage inflicted from a *New York Times* report, almost a year and a half after the war officially ended (i.e., on May 1, 2003), that

"Iraqi officials in charge of rebuilding their country's shattered and decrepit infrastructure [are] warning that the Bush administration's plan to divert $3.46 billion from water, sewage, electricity and other reconstruction projects to security could leave many people without the crucial services that generally form the backbone of a stable and functioning democracy."[15] The most optimistic estimates are that it will take perhaps a decade of stability and an investment of many billions of dollars to restore what has been destroyed. On the brighter side, the Paris Club, composed of 19 wealthy nations, has compassionately agreed to write-off 80 percent of the $38.9 billion that Iraq owed the club's members. This leaves the Iraqis owing only about $100 billion to other nations and to private investors,[16] an amount equal to about four times the nation's annual Gross Domestic Product.[17]

As of this writing, we have no hard data on Iraq's military and civilian casualties either during the actual war or during the first 20 months of the occupation. Given the swift dispersal and dissolution of the Iraqi army, military casualties were probably rather limited. Civilian deaths occasioned by the war and the occupation remain a matter of some controversy. *Lancet*, the British medical journal has calculated that there have been "100,000 excess [i.e., above normal death rates] civilian deaths after the Iraq invasion" but other estimates put the figure much lower, ranging from 15,000 to 17,500.[18] Most of the occupation-related Iraqi deaths have been due to insurgent (suicide bombers, etc.) activities[19] and, inevitably, the "counter-insurgency" measures taken by the occupying forces.[20]

The number of Iraqis *injured* as a consequence of the invasion and occupation is also unclear. The "normal" military ratio of injured to killed is usually about seven or eight to one. Whether that ratio holds among civilian casualties is uncertain and, as a further complication, we should remember that military medical care is probably much, much better than that lately available to most Iraqi civilians.

Afghanistan

The vast majority of civilian casualties here occurred during the period of intensive American bombing, running roughly from October 1, 2001 to March 1, 2002. Estimates of the number killed during this span run from 3,000 to 3,400;[21] a figure suggesting that there were also another 20,000 Afghanis injured. Since then, the number of those killed has probably risen by two or three hundred, and of those injured by at least another thousand.

The Gains

In both countries, harsh, despotic and—it seems safe to say—highly unpopular regimes have been overthrown. Both Afghanistan and Iraq have now had "reasonably" free and open national elections; in both, the people are much freer[22] in terms of what we might call the basic civil and political liberties.

However important the political gains, they are still sharply limited. The writ of the Afghanistan government carries little weight outside of Kabul; the Iraqi government still must rely on coalition troops to maintain even a modest semblance of law and order. In both countries, the current governments are essentially dependent on the occupying forces for their existence and both would quickly collapse should those forces be withdrawn. In neither is there yet that essential prerequisite to democracy—*a viable state* capable of providing, again to quote Fukuyama, "such basic, effectively functioning government institutions and services as armies, police forces, judiciaries, central banks, tax collection agencies, health and education systems, and the like" (2004a: 1).

At this juncture, we think, it would be most useful to focus our attention on Iraq. We say this for several reasons: Afghanistan has much the greater distance to go before it becomes a real, let alone a democratic, state in today's world; as noted above, it is one the world's lowest ranking countries, in terms of human development;[23] it is a much less important player in mid-Eastern politics and the U.S. government (more precisely, the present administration) is clearly prepared to invest far more heavily (as it already has) in Iraq than in Afghanistan;[24] weightiest of all, the invasion and occupation of this country has been and continues to be by far the more contentious (to understate the matter) political issue here at home. So . . .

As this is being written (late February, 2005), Iraq has successfully conducted its first ever national election. The Shiites (the Dawa Party) received 48 percent of the popular vote and earned 140 seats in the newly created 275 member National Assembly; the Kurdish Alliance took second place, winning 26 percent of the popular vote and 75 Assembly seats; ten other parties also won seats in the Assembly; but, a worrisome development, a sizable minority of Iraqis, the Sunnis, chose not to participate in the election. The major tasks of the Assembly will be (1) to select a prime minister; and (2) in ten months (i.e., by October 2005), to draft a new constitution.

So much for what has—or has not—been achieved. We now come to the key question: *As matters presently stand, what are the prospects for successful nation building in Iraq?*

Less foolhardy academics would [normally] reply, "It's too soon to tell." This response, however, would imply that we lack both the courage of our convictions and, even worse, faith in what we have insisted are the requisite *conditions*—given the nature of human nature—for the emergence and survival of a democratic polity. *To answer, then—The prospects are "very, very poor" if we are speaking of what can be accomplished during President Bush's*

*second term; they improve to no more than "very poor" if we stretch our time
horizon to a decade or so.*

Why such a bleak prognosis? To begin, Iraq still lacks most of the "requisite conditions" identified in chapter 4 as essential for a viable democracy; in fact, it is not clear whether the war and the occupation have improved or worsened matters in this respect. Second, the country continues to be plagued by deep-seated religious (Sunnis and Shiites) and ethnic (the Kurds) differences that so often preclude the political give-and-take essential in a democracy. Of themselves, these shortcomings alone would be sufficient grounds for pessimism but there is yet a third. As we emphasize in chapter 5 and its accompanying "operational checklist," there are quite a few requirements that the country *undertaking* nation building must satisfy—and the United States fails to meet many of them. Among them are an understanding of the peoples presumably being democratized and, perhaps most important of all, the readiness to make a very substantial investment of resources over a lengthy period of time. We lack both, especially the latter.

President Bush is proud of his readiness to "stay the course" in good causes or otherwise. Barring a major miracle, however, the continued need to pour money and American lives into Iraq may compel even someone so tenacious to realize that we now truly have a tiger by the tail. Albeit belatedly, that fact has already dawned on some of his fellow Republicans and, unless conditions in Iraq take a remarkable turn for the better, he is likely to face near-irresistible pressure from his own party, not to mention the Democrats, for an American exit well before the end of his second term. In fact, it would be an impressive achievement if the Iraqis manage to rebuild a *state*, in Fukuyama's sense of the term, let alone a democracy, during that time.

Nor are the prospects much brighter for a democratic Iraq a decade from now. Although the Iraqis will probably have managed to reestablish a state by then, we (and many of them) may not be altogether pleased by the form it will have taken. One needs only to look at what has happened in the countries that formerly constituted the Soviet Union to get some sense of the daunting obstacles that must be overcome [and the social, economic and political conditions that must be satisfied] before democracy becomes feasible.

In assessing what the "costs and consequences" of nation building we have to this point looked at Iraq and Afghanistan, the objects of this process. We turn now to our key concern, the gains and losses to the United States in its role as would-be nation builder.

The United States: Quite Another Set of Costs and Consequences

Over the past decade and a half, the United States has been involved in three nation building ventures. Since Haiti has already been discussed, we will focus here on our two most recent efforts, Afghanistan and Iraq. What have we accomplished—and at what price?

Gains

Granting that Afghanistan and Iraq were hardly major military powers, the speed and manner of their defeat were nonetheless truly impressive demonstrations—televised "live" around the world—of American military might. In the heady days immediately after the Iraq war, the United States was unquestionably seen not only as the most powerful nation in the contemporary world but possibly as one of the most powerful in history. Whether we are so regarded today, barely three years later, is a question to which we return a little later.

Second, our Iraqi nation building foray has inadvertently enriched American political electioneering. The 2004 campaign for the White House was probably the first in which a president, defending his decision to invade Iraq and his subsequent management of the ensuing occupation, advanced a claim of infallibility strikingly reminiscent of that once voiced by the Vatican. By so doing—and so successfully—he set a precedent surely envied by his predecessors and almost certain to be emulated by his successors.

Third, forced unexpectedly, reluctantly, and with dismayingly inadequate preparation into the role of occupying victor, we relearned what we had forgotten from our Vietnam experience—that is, that traditional weaponry, no matter how sophisticated, and conventional tactics, no matter how skilled, are no guarantee of victory in dealing with fanatical, determined, and totally ruthless "insurgents" or "terrorists," call them what we will.

We soon discovered that, as one critic put it, "[w]hen Vietnam ended, the Army didn't significantly change its way of operating. Instead, it was eager to return to its roots and prepare for more-conventional battle . . ." And it did. Describing a 1987 discussion at the Army's John F. Kennedy Special Warfare School, a visiting colonel bemusedly reported that "the old graybeard there told me that in 1975 he was told to get rid of the Vietnam stuff." [25] Just as King Canute presumably learned from the failure of the ocean to heed his command, American policy makers may benefit from the reminder that there are real limits to the ability of even a superpower to enforce its commands on a truly recalcitrant population. [26]

No discussion of "gains" would be complete without explicit acknowledgment that we "overthrew Saddam Hussein." Yes, we did and, on balance, it was undoubtedly a real gain—for the Iraqis. Whether it was, on balance, a gain for the United States is at least debatable. Since, as it now clear, there were no "Weapons of Mass Destruction" being amassed, how did we then benefit? True, one dictator less is probably a good thing, but there are still quite a few of them around, several arguably worse than

Saddam. Nor, as we will see, was his overthrow achieved without considerable cost—a subject to which we return shortly.

As the reader has already discerned, we have been hard-pressed to identify tangible, lasting benefits to the United States of its invasion and subsequent occupation of Afghanistan and Iraq. Of those we have identified, America's stature as *the* superpower has already been significantly diminished; the contribution to the armory of American political campaign tactics is not without its negative aspects; and the advantages of having ousted Saddam an open issue. Only the reminder that there are inherent limitations to power based primarily on military might is of real potential value. But, if history is any guide, this is likely, once again, to be soon forgotten.

Costs

In sharp contrast, there were some very substantial costs entailed in these two nation building efforts, costs that we should neither minimize nor ignore. We begin, accordingly, with the price we have paid so far—first in terms of lives, then of dollars.

Casualties

American military losses in the Afghanistan conflict, up to February 1, 2005, were some 150 killed and about 900 injured. The situation in Iraq, however, has been altogether different. Although we fortunately suffered few losses during the period of "formal" hostilities, the situation soon changed and the casualties began to mount, reaching some 1,500 killed, and about 11,000 wounded by the end of January 2005.[27] To these figures, of course, we should add the perhaps 100 plus American civilians killed or injured during this period.[28]

The Economic Cost

The fiscal price of democratizing Iraq is an extraordinarily elusive target because it involves juggling amounts appropriated and spent, those appropriated but not yet spent, and those requested but not yet appropriated. The situation is further muddled by the understandable desire of the administration and its supporters to minimize—and of those who oppose the administration's Iraq policy, to maximize—past, present, and projected expenditures. Then, there is the further difficulty of distinguishing between military and civilian reconstruction outlays, and between "regular" defense and Iraq related military expenditures, and so on. Still, allowing for some slippage in either direction,[29] a reasonably accurate estimate is that, by the close of 2004, our "mission in Iraq," to borrow a *New York Times'* euphemism, had already cost about $180–200 billion[30] to which should be added the president's request, in early February, 2005, for an additional $82 billion (of which perhaps 10 percent was for Afghanistan), giving a total of about $250 billion.[31] To put these figures into perspective, the outlay of the federal budget for fiscal 2003–2004 was $2.2 trillion (in 2005 dollars), with a resulting deficit of some $412 billion; comparable figures for fiscal 2004–2005 were $2.3 trillion in outlay and a projected deficit (the figure varies, depending whether one relies on the Congressional Budget Office or on the administration) of around $425 billion.[32] For 2006, President Bush has asked for a "skeleton" (i.e., *sans* the above mentioned $82 billion) $2.5 trillion.

Of itself, the $250 billion for nation building warrants no conclusion. Conceivably, the nation could be in such excellent economic and fiscal shape that it could easily afford the expenditure. It is quite another matter, though, when we are experiencing the large budget deficits[33] and when the purpose for which the $250 billion is being spent dangerously divides the nation[34] and diverts public attention and badly needed resources from addressing serious domestic problems—political, social, and economic problems which, if not resolved, threaten to jeopardize the long-term health of the American democracy. And it is these problems to which we now turn.

"Domestic" Consequences

Immediately above we spoke of "political, economic, and social." In actuality, of course, these three categories often overlap: "political" developments may well have "economic" repercussions; a "social" change may markedly alter the "economic" situation, and so on. This being the case, and given the somewhat greater difficulty of distinguishing the "social" from the "economic," we felt it would be better to organize our discussion under two, rather than three, headings—one, "political," the other "social and economic."

Political Costs

Beyond doubt, the controversies spawned by the Iraq war have underlined the shortcomings of our political system and, by aggravating already existing personal and political animosities, lessened the likelihood that these defects can or will be constructively addressed in the near future.

As the United States neared the end of the twentieth century, there was already a growing sense that the American polity, using that term to encompass the federal government's three "separate" branch (legislative–executive–judicial) structure, on the one hand, and our two party electoral system, on the other, was no longer really capable of meeting the increasingly complex problems besetting the nation.[35] These structural weaknesses, abetted by the widening ideological and personal differences between the parties, dogged the Clinton years and critically influenced the outcome of the presidential elections in 2000, decided by one vote in a Supreme Court unmistakably divided along partisan lines.

Although he had pledged to be a "unifier, rather than a divider," the early months of President Bush's administration, with what its opponents derisively termed a "welfare for the wealthy" program, hostility to abortion and stem cell research, antienvironmentalist bias, and ill-concealed contempt for Congress,[36] had the opposite effect. Although the "war on terrorism," triggered by the tragic events of "9/11" briefly brought the nation closer together, the manner in which that war was conducted by an administration admittedly more concerned with "national security" than with civil liberties or the Geneva Convention,[37] and quick to dismiss criticism as unpatriotic, soon revived and strengthened the old suspicions and hostilities.

Such was the political setting when the president launched his campaign for action against Iraq. It is this setting that explains, in large part, the anger elicited by the belated discovery, after our stunning military victory, that there were no WMDs; that the administration had not anticipated the possibility of a determined, ruthless, and bloody postwar insurgency and the resulting need for a prolonged American occupation; that it would take many, many billions to rebuild Iraq, democratic or not; and that United States, having scorned the UN in launching the war, could now expect little assistance from this quarter.

For all these reasons, the war with Iraq added fuel to already blazing partisan and ideological fires. Small wonder that the 2004 campaign was one of the nastiest in recent history. Still, however grave the domestic political consequences, they were probably less than the political damage suffered abroad. Nor, and this is our next concern, were they as potentially threatening to our democratic way of life as the concomitant economic and social costs.

Economic and Social Consequences

Few of the major social and economic problems currently facing the United States can be blamed on our nation building ventures. To be sure, cost of the Afghan and Iraqi "missions" added substantially to an already growing budgetary deficit, but this deficit had its origins in an economic downturn and the administration's tax cut policies. Almost all the other problems— poverty, inadequate low-income housing, unemployment, the environment, racism and discrimination, a deteriorating physical infrastructure (roads, railroads, water, sewage, electricity, etc.), sky-rocketing medical costs and inadequate health insurance coverage, a demographically endangered social security system, an increasingly parsimonious welfare safety net, rising prison populations, a public school system too often incapable of transmitting either knowledge or civic values, even the "war against terrorism"—to mention only some of the most serious concerns—antedate the (senior) Bush and Clinton administrations and, in many instances, those of their predecessors as well.

But though George W. Bush's nation building did not create these problems, it had three clearly adverse effects. Perhaps most important, it diverted attention from the need to take corrective action. During his first administration, practically no important legislation dealing with any of these problems was enacted. In the 2004 election, the wisdom of the president's resort to arms, and the relative capacities of the two candidates to deal with "terrorism" and to bring the occupation of Iraq (and to a lesser degree, of Afghanistan) to a successful conclusion, dominated the campaign. The first of the three heralded debates, and sizable segments of the other two dealt with those topics, and a persuasive case can be made that these were issues on which the outcome eventually turned.

The second consequence was that Iraq not only absorbed resources that might otherwise have been devoted to these problem areas but, given a tightening budgetary situation, often led to a cut in the funds they had previously received. Furthermore, since much of this money was intended as matching funds, grants in aid, etc. the cuts affected not only federal programs but also those at the state, county, and local levels.

As noted above, the cost of the two wars and the postwar occupations was projected to hit some $250 billion plus by the end of federal fiscal year 2005–2006. For a country where the number (35.9 million)[38] of those living below the poverty line ($18,600 for a family of four) rose from 12.1 percent in 2002 to 12.5 percent in 2003; where the proportion of children (those under 18) living in poverty went from 16.7 percent to 17.6 percent;[39] and where those without health insurance (45 million) increased from 19.5 percent to 20.2 percent,[40] this $250 billion, or any significant portion thereof, could more usefully have been invested elsewhere.[41]

In fact, an August 2004 "op-ed" piece in the *New York Times* laid out in some detail how the $140 billion spent up to that date in Iraq could (and by not overly subtle implication, should) have been spent on antiterrorist measures to "safeguard Americans." Alternatively, as *Newsday* pointed out, the money authorized to carry the Iraq occupation through 2004 would provide "a year's worth of medical care for 34 million people, or build 17,957 new schools." [42] We agree with the basic thrust of the two pieces: just as with charity, efforts to protect and nurture democracy should begin at home.[43]

Third, the distraction of attention and the diversion of resources have produced predictable consequences. In many of these problem areas, the situation has worsened over the intervening years. A larger proportion of the population—and of children—now lives below the poverty level. Our economy has barely regained the number of jobs lost during the recent economic turndown and many of the newly created positions are at lower salary levels than those eliminated. A creaking infrastructure has further deteriorated. Our 50,000 page federal tax code, whose complexity imposes an estimated $100 billion annual cost on the economy (almost as expensive as nation building), has become even longer and more arcane.[44] More Americans lack health insurance. The percentage of retirees and imminent retirees has risen thereby heightening the possibility of an eventual crisis in our Social Security system.[45] And, to cut the litany short, the current real estate "bubble" has made it even more difficult for lower-income families to purchase a home.

Individually, these are serious matters; collectively, they pose a growing threat to our national well being. Nonetheless, they could be tolerated for the present if there was good reason to think that they will be constructively addressed in the not too distant future. Unfortunately, with attention centered on Iraq and on "terrorism," nothing has been done to change a political system that, as discussed above, seems no longer able or willing to tackle major issues.[46] This alone would be bad enough. Worse, the prospects of successful action have been further diminished by the personal attacks and animosities, the open distrust, the ideological differences, and the "end justifies the means" tactics that have increasingly characterized relations between our major parties *and* between the so-called liberal and conservatives wings of the parties themselves. All in all, not a very heartening outlook.[47]

To this point, we have considered only the "domestic" consequences of American nation building in Iraq and Afghanistan. But our account would be grievously incomplete without some mention of the impact our actions have had on how we are perceived by other nations. For much of the world, the United States epitomizes democratic governance, and their view of us inevitably colors their attitude toward the latter. Though our sister democracies may find the statement a shade presumptuous, we exaggerate only slightly in saying that, for many people in many nations, "as America goes, so goes democracy."

It might be useful to draw the balance in terms of Machiavelli's memorable query about political power—"Is it better to be feared or loved?" Being Machiavelli, he (in)famously opted for fear—and that is where we will start.

On May 1, 2003, having reduced the Iraqi army to rabble and many of Iraq's cities to rubble, the United States was certainly the most feared nation on earth. Over the following months, however, this apprehensive regard was steadily lessened by our inability to establish more than a semblance of law and order; by an increasingly deadly insurgency that has claimed over 1,500 U.S. military, and many, many thousands of Iraqi civilian, lives; by the televised pictures of American soldiers and the civilians of many countries taken captive and executed by "terrorists." The lesson was not lost. American military might was irresistible at traditional warfare—but as for dealing with terrorists and insurgents, well, there was a king-sized Achilles heel.

Now for "love," a term that we will use to subsume "respect" and "admiration" as well. Whatever their initial views on the merits of the war itself, we undoubtedly lost many friends abroad by the manner in which we treated—or more precisely, were portrayed as treating—the prisoners captured in Afghanistan and then held incommunicado at "Gitmo" in Cuba.[48] But these losses were relatively trivial compared with the number estranged by the dubious case made to justify an invasion of Iraq[49] and the disregard for international opinion voiced by President Bush in the debates preceding the decision to attack. This decision, of course, was widely criticized and, in fact, opposed by sizable majorities even in the nations (Great Britain, Spain, Poland, and Australia)[50] that constituted the invading "coalition." Needless to say, the subsequent reluctant admission that there simply were no WMDs to be found did little to restore our credibility.

Nothing, though, damaged our reputation, and the esteem in which the United Sates was held, so much as the televised images of the degrading treatment of the Iraqi prisoners at Abu Ghraib[51] and, as further information became available, elsewhere. In the face of evidence this knowledge and tacit acceptance of this behavior ran far, far up the chain of command, that the Red Cross had previously expressed its concerns, that the administration had earlier taken a disturbingly narrow view of the Geneva Convention, and of our harsh handling of the Guantanamo prisoners,[52] the American excuse that these were the acts of a few "rogue" soldiers carried little conviction in the world at large[53] and considerably less in Moslem nations.[54]

To return to Machiavelli's dichotomy: what have been the consequences, in terms of international opinion, of our two recent exercises in nation building?[55] With regard to fear, whatever was gained during the war was probably dissipated by our mishandling of the occupation. As for "love," well, the question is best not asked.[56] Considering the consequences at home and abroad of our attempt to bring democracy to Afghanistan and to Iraq, we may well wonder whether both that cause and the United States itself may not have lost a great deal more than has been gained. As one observer sought to sum up the situation shortly after the Iraqi election

> Iraq is still a very, very long way from democracy. And even if it gets there, the costs of the journey—the more than ten thousand (so far) American wounded and dead, the tens of thousands of Iraqi men, women and children killed, the hundreds of billions of dollars diverted from other purposes, the lies, the distraction from and gratuitous extension of the "war on terror," the moral and political catastrophe of systematic torture, the draining of good will toward and sympathy for America, will not necessarily justify themselves. (Hertzberg, 2005: 98)

Chapter Eight
The Fourth "Whereas"

If we were to recast the case argued in the foregoing chapters as a formal resolution, it would look something like the following:

1. Whereas humans (i.e., *Homo sapiens*) are social primates and, like all social, are predisposed by their evolutionary history to live in hierarchically organized structures; and

2. Whereas, as a consequence, democratic polities (1) require special enabling for their birth and survival, conditions that need considerable time to develop and mature; are (2) fragile and relatively short-lived; (3) have been and continue even today, in the so-called Age of Democracy, to be very much a minority form of government; and

3. Whereas attempts to export democracy, that is, nation building, (1) with few exceptions have been markedly unsuccessful; and (2) where successful, have required substantial investments of time and resources by the state(s) making this attempt; and (3) the long-term success of democracy is closely tied to the health and viability of its major political exponent, the United States.

This bring us to the fourth "whereas"—which we believe can accurately and succinctly stated as:

4. Whereas the United States is currently experiencing severe political, economic, and social problems that require prompt attention and, in all probability, the investment of substantial resources before they do irreparable damage to the world's leading democracy.

It is these problems—and their implications for nation building policy—to which we turn to in this penultimate chapter. With the statement of this fourth "Whereas," we will have completed the case for our "Therefore Be It Resolved . . ." proposals regarding future nation building policy.

To reassure the understandably uneasy reader, we have no intention of presenting a lengthy litany of what ails America. Some of these difficulties, however serious they may be, are less immediately threatening—in terms of their potential damage to our democratic polity—than those we will be discussing. For that reason, we will not talk about: racism, sexism, and ethnic friction;[1] the homeless and the worsening shortage of low-income housing;[2] the unrelieved threats to our physical environment; the deterioration of our roads, bridges, transportation, and utility systems; a Social Security system endangered by changing demographic patterns, on the one hand, and by proposals to privatize it on the other;[3] a penal system that puts more citizens behind bars for longer periods (and alone practices capital punishment) than does any "First World" nation;[4] the present and longer-term implications of job "outsourcing" and the replacement of well-paid skilled positions with minimum wage, often part-time employees; a health care system that leaves 20 percent[5] of our population unprotected, and with steadily rising costs passed on, where possible, to those who are uninsured;[6] a federal tax system that seems primarily designed to provide a steady flow of students to university programs in accountancy and law; and, as a last example, not even about a federal fiscal policy, apparently based on the recent revelation that "deficits don't matter," practically ensuring budgetary shortfalls for the next decade or so.

All of these are real problems that, if not addressed, have the potential for grave long-term consequences. But they are not as urgent, we think, as the threat to the American democracy posed by four interrelated developments: (1) the growing incidence of poverty and the unequal distribution of wealth in our society; (2) a political system, originally designed to slow down, rather than facilitate governmental action, now increasingly sclerotic in its attempts to deal with twenty-first-century issues; (3) a dangerous loss of that difficult to define but absolute essential for effective democratic governance—"social capital"; and (4) an educational system that, aside from other major shortcomings, is no longer capable of a task that it once performed superbly—democratic civic indoctrination.

None of these developments, we should hasten to say, was caused by nation building. Some, however, were worsened by the diversion of resources which, had we not gone to war with Iraq and Afghanistan, *might* have been directed toward their correction; all, certainly, suffered from the distraction of attention triggered by the decision to invade Iraq and the acrimonious, ongoing disputes spawned by this decision. In an earlier chapter we tried to assess the costs to the United States of the Afghanistan and Iraqi wars. Following the lead of the economists, we should not overlook the possibly even greater costs to the United States of the problems consequently *not* addressed.

Nor, we should also emphasize, would any of these problems be significantly alleviated, let alone "cured," by the abandonment of our nation building ambitions. True, one of them (poverty) might benefit from the resulting "freeing up" of federal funds[7] but, in reality, they are all too complex and too deep seated for additional funding alone to be a panacea. The real benefit, instead, would be from a long-overdue shift of national attention from seeking to establish democracy elsewhere to the far more important task of strengthening and preserving it here at home. Given the inherent fragility of democratic governance, and of the special conditions required for both its birth and survival, this is a task that has been too long neglected.

Now, for a quick survey of the four developments which, we think, currently pose the most serious threats not only to the health but also to the longevity of the American republic as we now know it.

Poverty—And Wealth

True, the New Testament warns that "the poor ye shall always have with you." But nowhere does it mandate that their number should increase—as has been happening in this country.

To start with a few familiar, if unwelcome, statistics: At the close of 2003, four decades after Lyndon Johnson launched his heralded "war on poverty," some 35.9 million (i.e., 12.5 percent) of Americans, up from 34.8 million (12.1 percent) the previous year, are living below the official poverty levels of an annual income of $18,800 for a family of four, $14,680 for a family of three, $12,015 for a couple, and $9,393 for an "unattached individual." These levels are set by the U.S. Census Bureau and presumably represent the minimum income required to provide the basic necessities of shelter, food, clothing, and so on, although many experts in this area maintain that the basic necessities actually require a considerably larger income. Be that as it may—and we personally agree with the critics—the number of families living in official poverty was 7.6 million (10.0 percent), up from 7.2 million (9.6 percent) a year earlier. The number of children (those under 18) so classified was 12.9 million (17.6 percent) a jarring increase above the 12.1 million (16.7 percent) the previous year.[8] The poverty rate for "minorities" was 22.5 percent for Hispanics, 24.4 percent for blacks, and 11.8 percent for Asians; the first two were unchanged, the last up from 10.1 percent, the year before.[9] One point should be kept in mind here: as might be expected, some of those classified as impoverished were unemployed for one reason or another. But since many jobs pay less than a poverty level wage, many millions were members of what are termed "low income working families."[10]

To round out the picture: the number and rate of those living in poverty has risen for the past three years. In 2003 "the top 5% of households received 21.4 percent of our national income (up from 16.6 percent in 1973) while that of the lowest 20% declined to 3.4% in 2003 from 3.5% the year before."[11] And, as a final factoid, and in striking contrast with the various poverty level figures, the median American household income in 2003 was $43,318.[12]

So much for income. The data on wealth, as we know, reflect even greater disparities. In 2001, 59.2 percent of the nation's wealth was held by the top 5 percent of the population. Two years later, the top 1 percent owned 31 percent of the nation's total financial assets, 53 percent of the stocks, and 64 percent of the bonds (over this same period, the gap in wealth between whites and minorities continued to widen: by 2003, whites were ten times wealthier, on average, than Hispanics and blacks[13]). By the close of 2003 the United States had 2.27 million millionaires (one in every 125 Americans) who collectively owned approximately 31 percent of the nation's total financial assets, 53 percent of the stocks, and 64 percent of the bonds—"the starkest such concentration of wealth among industrialized countries."[14]

A frequent reaction to data describing the extent of poverty (and of staggering economic inequality) in the United States is the observation that "the poor in America live as well, and sometimes much better, than do the 'middle classes' in many other countries." True, but essentially irrelevant. Poverty is not only an "objective" condition, determined by measurable income, but a "subjective" state of mind, greatly influenced by how we perceive our situation compared with that of others and, perhaps still more, by our own aspirations. Few societies deliberately encourage such far-reaching economic and social aspirations as does ours. The media, and especially television with its incessant attention to "lives of the rich and famous," make it impossible for the impoverished to be unaware of the vast chasm between their marginal mode of existence and the luxurious lives of their more successful fellow Americans.[15] As Daniel Bell warned a quarter-century ago, no democratic society that fails to satisfy the hopes it has evoked, "can expect to ride out the consequent whirlwind in a comfortable fashion" (1976: 179), especially a society in which aspirations were set in the closing decades of the twentieth century, during what Robert Samuelson (1996) has aptly termed "the age of entitlement."[16]

Although, happily, there are many, many exceptions, poverty has a troublesome tendency to be self-perpetuating, even in our upwardly mobile American society. Although there are many other contributing causes (racial and ethnic prejudice, for example), two in particular play key roles—birth rate and education. By and large, the former correlates inversely with income: the higher the birth rate, the lower the family income.

Education is even more important. Other factors being equal, children from very poor families have less of an opportunity (and for cultural reasons, often little desire) to go on to higher education.[17] But education, as we know, "is a major determinant of both poverty rates and the growth of inequality. The median earnings of those with a high-school diploma or less have declined over the past 25 years, while those with college and graduate degrees have seen a sharp increase" (*The Economist*, October 9, 2004: 13). To an increasingly troublesome degree, the jobs available for those with minimal education or lacking special skills often pay less than poverty level hourly rates and carry very few benefits.

Here we face a twofold task: First, to make it financially possible for those who wish to do so, and who have the requisite ability, to achieve the education they desire; second, to awaken this desire. The former is surely feasible in a nation as wealthy as America; in fact, though there remains a goodly distance to go, we have already made considerable progress toward this goal (although one of the first acts of the post-2004 election House of Representatives was to approve a bill eliminating Pell grants for some 100,000 students). But the latter, that is, changing mindsets and inculcating the desire, is quite another matter.

This chapter, to repeat, looks at the developments in our society that pose real threats to the long-term welfare of our democracy. Among the most serious of these, we believe, is the growing number and proportion of Americans whose incomes fall beneath the officially designated "poverty" level and, no less troublesome, the widening difference between those at the top and those at the lower reaches of the wealth pyramid. In both past and recent times, large-scale poverty and the consequent internecine political struggle between the "haves" and the "have-nots"[18] have been major factors in the decline and fall of democratic polities. They gravely, perhaps fatally, weakened Athens in its losing rivalry with Sparta; sometimes turning into civil war, they were probably the determining factor in the demise of the Roman Republic; over the past century or so, they have led to the collapse of democratic governments in Latin America, Europe, and Asia. Not surprisingly, for those who are hungry, bread is usually more highly valued than the ballot. As reported earlier in this volume, recently asked to choose between economic betterment and democracy, a majority of Latin Americans expressed a decided preference for the former.

One-sixth of Americans (and an even larger proportion of children) now live below the poverty line; by and large, they live in cramped but costly (given their income) housing. With luck, they do not go hungry—or cold—too often. Only a minority have access to affordable medical (let alone to dental) care, other than that available at hospital emergency rooms. Over the past few years they have experienced a marked attenuation in the social services provided by the federal, state, and local governments. And, although many of them are employed, a large proportion do not earn enough to rise above the poverty line, or have sufficient financial resources to carry them on more than a week to week—or for the more fortunate—month to month basis.

They live, however, in what is still the world's most affluent society. Even the most impoverished have television and see an occasional motion picture; almost all of them can read. They are pretty well informed, consequently, about the standard of living enjoyed by their more fortunate fellow Americans and have read about and seen for themselves the luxuries taken for granted not only by those who, as viewed by private banks, are really rich (say, a net worth of $50 million and up) but by those who are merely affluent (say, just a few million dollars). The media also have made them increasingly aware (though to what degree we do not know) that their lack of education or special skills[19] limits their own chances of economic betterment—and possibly that of their children as well.

But they do have one important potential political asset—numbers.[20] Numbers enough, in fact, to tilt a national election one way or another. In the 2004 presidential campaign, Senator Kerry explicitly appealed to the economic interests of the "middle class," contrasting them with those of the "wealthy," allegedly favored by his opponent. Mr. Kerry might have done better had he widened his horizons (and campaign promises) and also directed an appeal to the 35 million Americans for whom anything approaching a middle class income would be a huge upward step. The potential of this tactic, utilized with striking success by Huey Long during the Great Depression, was fictionally explored by Sinclair Lewis and most recently, in a "what might have happened" novel, by Philip Roth.[21] We cannot discount the danger that it may be successfully employed here in the United States, just as it has been in other countries, by candidates and parties more eager to win office than to preserve democracy.

Of the four problem areas, poverty is the one probably most susceptible to amelioration by restoring and even expanding governmental services providing for the poor what they cannot readily secure for themselves. Even half the estimated $250 billion spent on invasion and occupation of Iraq could have made a meaningful difference in the quality of life for millions of low-income families. Regrettably, this is not likely to happen. If the 2004 election results are an indication, today's operative political motto to be "billions for defense, not once cent for poverty."

Absent a radical shift in the our political values and/or a business boom of near-unprecedented scope (with a substantial "trickling down" of economic benefits), there is little likelihood of a sizable decrease in the number of those falling below the poverty line or of an appreciable improvement in their standard of living. Of course, the poor we shall always have with us. But in a democracy as wealthy as ours, large scale poverty (one-sixth of the nation) is a near-irresistible invitation to demagogues and demagoguery.

The American Political System: The Patient is Not Improving

Innumerable books have been written on the defects and shortcomings of the American political system. From the perspective of its critics, these start with an inherently undemocratic and increasingly dysfunctional three-branches of government constitutional structure,[22] and go on to include our two-party system, the manner in which candidates are selected, the nature of American campaigns,[23] Congress and the legislative process, the role of the judiciary in setting policy, the growth (or decline) of presidential power, the relationship between "special interests" and the bureaucracy, and so on. Obviously, there is no way we can discuss all of these topics and the literature they have generated. With necessity again being the mother of brevity, we will accordingly focus on those that pose, as we see it, the most formidable and immediate threat to our democratic way of life—money in politics, the role of the media, and the continuing, possibly even accelerating, erosion of that admittedly amorphous and intangible good, "social capital."

Money in American Politics

To start with a handful of truisms—money plays an important role in the outcome of elections. The outcome of elections plays a very important role in the setting of public policy. Those who provide the money not unreasonably expect that their views will be heard and their interests given decent consideration. These expectations are usually fulfilled. In fact, as Elizabeth Drew (1999) has warned, probably the single most striking feature of American politics the past few decades has been the "vast, relentless takeover" of politics and policy making in this country by large donors to federal campaigns.

Allowing for a few exceptions, it is not so much personal venality that drives this process but rather the skyrocketing costs of gaining office, that is, of being nominated and then of winning the election. And the costs go steadily higher. Expenditures during the 2004 congressional and presidential elections ran an estimated $3.9 billion, up by about 30 percent from the 2000 total; the presidential race alone entailed a $1.2 billion outlay. Nor do Congressional seats come cheaply. Although the figure naturally varies from situation to situation, members of the House, on average, must raise at least $50,000 per week to finance a bid for reelection; their opponents will need an equivalent or even larger amount. The quest for a Senate seat is even more expensive, since these campaigns stretch across an entire state rather than a comparative small district.

The imperative for funds is felt by both (given the "normal" two major party race) candidates but, since the incumbents are usually favored for reelection, their appeals for financial support are likely to be more persuasive. There is a nice circularity operative here: This demonstrably superior ability to raise funds has long been recognized as one of the major reasons (gerrymandered districts also help) why incumbency is such a great advantage.[24] In 2004, for example, 435 House seats were theoretically at stake. Early in October, *The Economist* predicted that "incumbent congressmen of both parties have nothing to worry about . . . only 29 of the 435 House races are considered competitive." Close, but not quite on the mark. As matters turned out, 33 races (fewer than 10 percent) were fairly tight.[25] Superior fund-raising ability was also an asset when neither contestant is an incumbent: "In eight out of ten races for open seats in the House and in nine of ten open Senate races, the winners outspent their rivals."[26] Although it would be inaccurate to say that those who pay the piper invariably call the tune, their wishes are not often totally disregarded in deciding what music will be played.

In theory, there are three possible ways we might reduce, if not eliminate, the corrosive role of money in American politics. One is to lower the cost of running for office. Since the price of the elements entering into this cost— media time, advertising, communications, consultants, polling, organizational salaries, and so on—are essentially set by the market, this is hardly a promising line of attack. The second is public funding, which would presumably give a more level playing field. This is currently available but with so many strings attached that both Mr. Bush and Mr. Kerry decided otherwise. Their decision "saved taxpayer money but made the two main candidates even more dependent on the 'bundlers,' the fundraisers who specialize in racking up hundreds of $20,000 contributions."[27] Limiting the amount of money a candidate (or a party) can spend in a given campaign has been tried but, as the figures cited above testify, with limited success. Third, there could be limits on campaign contributions and the purposes for which they may be spent. Legislation presumably aimed at these ends has been repeatedly enacted (the McCain–Feingold bill being the most recent "reform") with as yet uncertain results.

The difficulty, we know, is not the absence of feasible solutions; other countries have done much better in this respect. It is, rather, that those who receive and those who give have combined to effectively block every attempt to enact really strict controls and limits. As matters presently stand, our two major parties do almost equally well at fund-raising; both have developed effective methods for working within (or getting around) the present legal constraints; and neither is quite sure whether it will gain or lose by a radical change in the present system. As the folk wisdom goes, "the devil known . . ." On the other side of the equation, those who provide the funds have every reason to value the return on their investments and are understandably resistant to any legislation that might endanger their present privileged position.

Would more effective controls on campaign expenditures and campaign contributions end the influence of "special interests" on the policy-making (and, we should add, policy executing) process? By no means. There are too many other ways for those who have the desire and the resources to pursue this objective. It might, however, appreciably lessen their influence—an urgently needed corrective. If public opinion surveys are taken at face value, Americans are increasingly skeptical about the workings of their government—and in a democracy there are few more alarming developments (e.g., Dalton, 2002, 2004; Pharr, Putnam, and Dalton, 2001).[28]

The News Media

No discussion of American politics would be complete without the mandatory critique of the media[29] for the part they have played in lowering the level of political discourse and debasing the electoral process.[30] We are all familiar with the bill of particulars—the emphasis, especially in television and radio, on the "30-second bite"; the focus on "who's ahead" rather than on substance; the pressure to be first with a story and a lesser concern with its accuracy; the fascination with personalities and with what was once regarded as the private lives of candidates; the simplification of complex problems and issues; in short, as almost all observers agree, a shift from serious journalism to entertainment.[31] The accusation that the "the United States cannot have a sensible campaign as long as it is built around the news media"[32] may overstate the matter—but not by much.

This attack on the media actually raises three overlapping issues. To begin, have we actually reached a new low in the level of political discourse and in the manner in which our political campaigns are conducted? Have rational arguments and intellectually coherent appeals to the voter been largely replaced by mudslinging, misrepresentation, and a casual disregard for both logic and fact? Second, if so, is it fair to hold the media primarily responsible? And, third, if so, what might be done?

To tackle the first question: we are constantly reminded of the vast gap between the Lincoln–Douglas debates, on the one hand, and the quality of the presentations made by the candidates in recent presidential debates, on the other. No doubt the difference is like day and night. Still, holding in abeyance the nit-picking objection that their debates occurred in the course of a senatorial rather than a presidential contest, were the Lincoln–Douglas exchanges really representative of the general level of American campaigning then, before then, or in the century and a half that has since elapsed? Even a casual reading of American political history suggests otherwise. By no later than 1800, the record makes clear, party campaign strategists were employing "no holds barred" tactics that would have elicited the professional admiration and approval of even the most amoral of our contemporary political consultants. The most persuasive case that can be made, then, is that the intellectual and ethical quality of our political campaigns has significantly declined in recent years, leaving unresolved whether we have managed a new low.

To turn to the second issue, are the media primarily responsible for this decline? Perhaps, even probably—but with a plausible plea of "extenuating circumstances."

The accusation against the news media is essentially the same as that levied against the media generally—that they deliberately pander to the lowest common denominator of taste in radio, motion pictures, television, and publishing and, that, by so doing, lower the level still further. To which the standard media responses are (1) it ain't so; (2) if we are to survive, that is, be profitable, we must give the public what it wants; (3-a) we would gladly do better but since our competitors will not . . .; and (3-b) we are in the entertainment business, not in public education.

To return to the case at hand: Are the news media, and their quest for the largest possible audience, responsible for dumbing down political campaigns—or are they simply responding to the public's positive response to this type of reporting—and campaigning? Although most critics have seized on the first explanation, they may be overestimating the tastes, the educational background, and the intellectual sophistication of a sizable segment of our population. Surely, this latter possibility should not be ignored. For instance, according to a recently published study, "[D]uring the 2000 debates George W. Bush and Al Gore spoke, respectively, at a sixth- and a high seventh-grade level (the Lincoln–Douglas debates were carried out at about a twelfth-grade level.) And the Bush–Gore contest actually marked a slight uptick after almost two decades of decline."[33]

The third issue, of course, is what can be done to improve the quality of our nation's political reportage and, by so doing, strengthen a malfunctioning political system? As indicated above, we think that *both* the news media's "entertain first, inform later" approach to elections, and the failure of our schools adequately to prepare our young for democratic citizenship, must be held accountable. We consider the former factor next but postpone the latter for a subsequent discussion of American civic education.

To start with what may be the root of the problem: There is really no persuasive evidence that any vast proportion of Americans are notably unhappy with the kind of treatment most news media give to politics generally and election campaigns in particular. Yes, the "chattering classes" are critical but, almost by definition, there is rarely a close fit between the views of this group and those of the public at large. Granted, opinion surveys sometimes report negative views of the news media—but many respondents are not unaware that such expressions are now intellectually quite fashionable. Against these survey results there is the cold, hard fact[34] that this is the kind of coverage the media (whose survival and profitability turn on their ability accurately to judge public taste) believe appeals the most to their audiences.

There are two additional factors operating to encourage rather than discourage this development. One is that, ever seeking to expand their audience, the media continue to blur the line between news and entertainment, with the latter increasingly becoming more important. As a result, we have a spate of "news programs" characterized by a frankly one-sided (i.e., liberal or conservative) "interpretation" of political events or, in a parody of even-handedness, by two or three "journalists" presumably representing divergent viewpoints but disconcertingly alike in their readiness to interrupt in mid-sentence, to ignore inconvenient facts or ideas, and unhesitatingly to resort, knowingly or otherwise, to practically any or all of the known logical fallacies. The other factor operative is that programs emphasizing local news draw larger audiences, and hence are more attractive to advertisers, than those focusing primarily on the national and international scene. The kind of thoughtful, critical political analysis retrospectively associated with such legendary figures as Walter Cronkite, Chet Huntley and David Brinkley, Edward R. Murrow, and Howard K. Smith apparently does not compete very well for public attention with the antics of the city council, another odorous failure of the new (and far over budget) sewage system, or the degree of nudity to be permitted at the town beaches or at the establishments offering "adult entertainment."

Under these circumstances, it would be truly Utopian to expect any marked voluntary improvement in political reporting from the media themselves. At worst, critics will be ignored; at best, emulating the strategy honed by the radio, television, and motion picture industries when the complaints about the quality of programming become too numerous and shrill to be ignored, there will be the familiar mix of denials, mea culpas, and fervent promises to do better in the future.[35] While, fortunately, there still remain a small handful of newspapers and magazines able and willing to swim against the tide, given the consolidation taking place in the publishing world, and the decreasing percentage of Americans who rely primarily on the printed word for their news, their number is more likely to shrink than to expand.

There is, of course, the (somewhat remote) possibility that an improvement in campaign coverage—and a commensurate gain in the intellectual level of American politics—might be sparked by a popular reaction against the present emphasis on trivia and a demand for a more substantively oriented reportorial approach. Should that occur, the media will no doubt comply as quickly as feasible. The obvious question, of course, is what could trigger such a demand? For that we have no answer other than that mass tastes are notoriously fickle—as the boom and bust of quiz shows, talk shows, "reality" shows, "poker" shows, and "survival" shows testify. Still, though it may be heartening to hope that public preferences might change, there is always the danger that the change may not be for the better.

Rather than rely on an admittedly unlikely occurrence, we might consider a more proactive policy—and at least explore the possibility of publicly funded radio and television programming and news reportage modeled on the British Broadcasting Corporation rather, than is presently the case, on our own grudgingly subsidized National Public Radio and Television Corporation. Despite the embarrassments it experienced this past year, the BBC, if not quite "the greatest force for cultural good on the face of the earth," (*This Week*, December 17, 2004: 8), provides a news service, and a quality of national and international political reporting, which has few peers. A "United States Broadcasting Corporation" variant of the BBC might improve the quality of American radio and television journalism in at least two ways. First, by setting a standard, especially if it attracted a demographically desirable audience, with which the commercial media would have to compete.[36] Second, it would provide a sort of benchmark against which those who, though usually preferring a more popularized treatment could, when so motivated, check the information they were (or possibly were not) receiving from other sources.

To be sure, the United States is not Great Britain. What has worked well in a nation where "socialist" is not an epithet may not function as hoped in a nation where "liberal" is. Nor are we proposing an adoption of the BBC model, lock, stock, and barrel. Beyond doubt, and learning from the experience of NPR and NPT, an American variant would probably be more akin to a cousin than to a sibling. In the final analysis, though, our options seem to be quite limited: we can wait and hope that the media will voluntarily raise the level of American political journalism—or we might give serious thought to some mechanism that might possibly impel them in that direction. Of the two, the latter might be the more rewarding policy.

The Erosion of Social Capital

Few political developments have greater potential for damage to the American democracy than the erosion of what social scientists call "social capital."[37] Rather than attempt a precise definition, it might be more useful

to identify the major elements which, most students agree, collectively constitute "social capital": (1) a general acceptance of and agreement on a body
of basic political beliefs and values—and a widely held conviction that even
those with whom one differs on specific issues, share these basic beliefs and
values; (2) a willingness to "play by the rules"—and the belief that even
those with whom one disagrees politically share that willingness; (3) a readiness, albeit sometimes reluctant, to compromise, even on important
issues—and the belief that those with whom one disagrees also share this
readiness; (4) a willingness to accept political defeat, even on important
matters, and still continue to work amicably with one's political opponents—and the belief that one's political opponents also share this willingness; and (5) a willingness to conduct political campaigns primarily in terms
of issues, rather than by focusing largely on the alleged personal weaknesses
and shortcomings of one's opponents—and the belief that one's political
opponents share this willingness.

All governments, even totalitarian states, require some measure of social
capital if they are to survive and function—and among the various forms
that polities take, none more so than democracies, which almost by definition depend primarily on shared values, popular acceptance, and a widespread sense of "legitimacy." We need hardly belabor the point. If we take
the above five criteria at all seriously, the conduct of American politics in
recent decades—especially the past few years—suggests our national stock
of social capital has been eroded to the point where, if we are to continue as
a democracy, it is in dangerously short supply. The first truly troublesome
signs of this erosion became apparent during the 1960s, a decade characterized by profound disagreements over the civil rights movement and over
the Vietnam war. Then, in the early 1970s, there was Watergate; during the
1980s, the still-controversial Reagan administration; in the 1990s, the
embattled Clinton years; and, viewed from today's perspective, George W.
Bush's even more divisive first term. Each, with the cumulative effect of a
Chinese water torture, further depleted a diminishing stock of political
goodwill.

As the reader knows, there is already a large, rapidly expanding, bitterly
polemic and fundamentally disheartening literature that addresses the manner in which, for those concerned with the future of the American democracy, our political climate changed markedly for the worse.[38] Rather than to
retrace the now-familiar ground, it might be more useful to ask—What
might be done to slow, to halt, and then if we are fortunate, even to reverse
this potentially destructive development?

The first step, we would say, is to convince the public at large and their
Congressional representatives that we have here the makings of a very serious problem. To be sure, over the past few years an alarm to this effect has

been voiced by a number of the contributors to our "more intellectually oriented" media. These media, however, reach a relatively small audience and it is doubtful that the general public is either aware of these concerns or, if aware, regards them to be anything other than expected exaggerations of disgruntled "sore losers." Although we are probably safe in treating it as a concern now held by a sizable segment of the chattering classes, we really do not know the extent to which it is shared by those outside this relatively limited circle.

Fortunately, we do have a technology capable of addressing that issue. A well-designed public opinion survey could cast light not only on extent to which social capital has been depleted but on the specific areas of belief where the erosion has been the greatest and the specific subsets of population (geographic, economic, ethnic, etc.) that have been most adversely affected. Such a survey could serve three distinct purposes: (1) to indicate the extent to which the loss of social capital constitutes a real problem; and if so, (2) to identify specific areas of belief, and the specific subpopulations, in which there has been the greatest attrition; and (3) by so doing, to suggest possible lines of corrective action.

There are three problematic aspects to this proposal of which we need take note. First, survey responses, especially on sensitive issues, may give an incomplete or even erroneous, data. True—but a well-designed survey still provides the best tool we presently have available. Second, what agency should conduct the survey? We would propose that it be done by one of the top-ranked universities or by commercial survey organizations, rather than by a governmental agency. Third, who will pay for it? (Perhaps this should have been the first question.) Ideally, the federal government, although there is little reason to think that those (in both parties) who benefit from the status quo would be enthusiastic supporters. More realistically, it could easily be funded by any of the half-dozen of our major foundations. And on that optimistic note . . .

Education for Democratic Citizenship: The More Serious Failure

Few aspects of contemporary American society have come under such broad and sustained criticism as our public schools. Writing almost a decade ago, we called attention to what a vast literature described, in essence, as "the failures of our educational system and the functional illiteracy of so many high school and even college graduates."[39] If the studies that have since been published are an accurate indicator, not much seems to have changed. The public schools, many stubbornly resistant to change, are still not doing well.[40] Black students, for reasons about which there remain sharp differences of opinion, are still doing worse than their white peers.[41]

American fourth-graders have slipped from 12th to 25th in the global ranking when tested in math and science;[42] and American teens rank 24th in
mathematics when compared with their peers in 28 other countries.[43]

From our perspective, however, the alleged academic shortcomings of
our schools are far less important than their manifest inability (or unwill-
ingness) to do what they once managed so superbly—civic indoctrination.
This is not a term, we realize, to be casually employed in a society enamored
of political correctness. Nonetheless, like it or not, all polities must inculcate in their young a belief in the virtues of the existent political order; in
almost every country, the primary responsibility for this task is assigned to
the educational system.[44] As France's President Chirac recently observed,
the students' concept of "France" and "idea of citizenship" is "an identity
forged in the neutral space of its public school" (Kramer, 2004: 66).
Unfortunately, this task is rarely undertaken, let alone effectively accomplished, in the American public school system, an omission that may well
be a major factor in the erosion of social capital discussed above.

Writing in 1997, we were reasonably optimistic that this situation could
be corrected without a radical change in an educational system organized on
a federal basis, where each state establishes its own educational requirements; in fact, just how this could be accomplished was to be the subject of
our next book. After a year of seeking to devise a method whereby this could
be done, our optimism began to evanesce. Today, looking at the diverse
directions—some forward, some backward, and many not at all—in which
literally thousands of state and local boards of education are moving, we
have become reluctantly convinced that a national policy, set by Congress,
will be required if our schools are again to undertake the task of "forging" a
sense of American civic identify. Put bluntly, education for democratic citizenship in this country is simply too important a matter to be left to the dis-
cretion of the individual states.

Objections? No shortage, surely. The first is that it is not the proper
function of the schools to teach citizenship, not even democratic citizenship. This is an objection to which we have responded in some detail elsewhere;[45] all we can do here is agree to disagree. Next, that there is the danger
that civic education might turn into uncritical indoctrination. It certainly
could, and to minimize this danger, we have proposed the following guidelines (Somit and Peterson, 1997: 114):

1. To ensure that students are given a basic understanding of American
   history and the manner in which our governmental system functions.
   These subjects are already part of the curricula of most of our schools,
   but numerous studies indicate that students too often complete their
   education incredibly ill-informed on both these areas. The goals here

would be to improve, where necessary, the content and quality of what are generally termed "civics" courses and to inculcate in the students a favorable but by no means uncritical perception of democracy in general and the American democracy in particular.

2. To convey an understanding of the history of democracy and democratic theory, of the difference not merely of political form but of substantive political life between authoritarian and democratic governments, of the special problems faced by democracies, and, consequently, of their unique fragility. This material should not be taught in terms of abstract political concepts but should be directly related to current issues faced by the United States and, where relevant, to other contemporary democratic polities.

Third, there are those who concur that our schools can and should be the vehicle for civic education but who insist that responsibility for this should remain with the states, not shifted to the federal government. Although that de facto arrangement worked very nicely in the nineteenth and early twentieth centuries; it has since almost completely fallen by the wayside. Much as we would prefer to believe otherwise, we do not think it possible to turn the clock back. Influential as are the special interest lobbyists in Washington, they seem to be even more persuasive in the state capitols. The end result, we fear, is likely be a multitude of policies—or no policy at all.

Another predictable and legitimate objection is that it would take a long time for such a policy to show positive results. No—and yes. "No," because the attempt to formulate and put such a policy into effect would quickly give rise to a national debate over how—and possibly even whether—the proposed results could be best achieved. Such a debate, calling national attention to what we think is a very urgent problem, would of itself serve a constructive end. "Yes," because it would necessarily be several years after the policy had actually been implemented before we would begin to see the results among our young adults in terms of a better informed, more intellectually critical—but much positively oriented—American civic spirit. We would all prefer to see a speedier response but a substantial lag time is simply another aspect of the price we must now pay for our failure to correct this situation decades ago.

Finally, some might object that such a policy would not be successful, that schools are not capable of accomplishing democratic education that have meaningful results. The literature testifies otherwise. For instance, active political participation is important in a democracy. Research indicates that adult civic education actually enhanced citizens' political involvement in the Dominican Republic and in South Africa (Finkel, 2002).

A wide-ranging survey of research in democratic education shows that across many different societies, such efforts can make a difference (Ichilov, 2003).[46]

Growing poverty and widening economic inequality in an extraordinarily affluent society; a political system increasingly incapable of satisfactory governance; a grievous loss of social capital; and the failure of our schools to prepare our young for effective, democratic citizenship—*these are the urgent problems facing and, we submit, threatening the American democracy. These are the problems that, above all, should determine our policy priorities and our political agenda.*

CHAPTER NINE

"THEREFORE BE IT RESOLVED . . .":
TOWARD MORE REALISTIC FOREIGN AND
DOMESTIC POLICIES

Few readers who have followed (and possibly even agreed with) our argument to this point will be greatly surprised by the two "resolutions" to
which we think it inexorably leads. The first, of course, is "that the U.S.
should not attempt nation building in the future unless careful study indicates the presence of most, if not all, of the requisite 'enabling conditions' in
both the target nation *and* in this country"; The second is "that the U.S. can
best further the cause of democracy world-wide by devoting its attention,
energies and resources to resolving the political, social and economic problems that increasingly threaten the future of democratic government here at
home." Having already presented the evidence and reasoning that led us to
these resolutions, we should next try to anticipate some of the questions and
objections they are likely to elicit.

Clearly, we should tackle the *big* question at the outset. *What, of possible
value, have we been able to contribute to an already much debated issue?* As our
references and citations testify, a number of social scientists have argued
against nation building. Some, after analyzing previous attempts, have
warned that nation building is rarely successful; others have stressed the
demanding variety of conditions that must be satisfied if this objective is
to be achieved. Nonetheless, as authors are prone to do, we have persuaded
ourselves that we have made two potentially useful contributions—the
first essentially practical, the second "theoretical"—to what has previously
been said.

At the practical level, borrowing enthusiastically and unstintingly from
the work of others, we have developed two "checklists" that we think can be
quite helpful in bringing together the information essential for a sound
decision. But "decision" is probably not quite the proper term, since such
checklists are most often utilized at the staff level in preparing recommendations and outlining possible courses of action. As we know, the actual

decisions—though frequently influenced by staff studies—are normally made at higher levels and are often influenced less by the evidence compiled in checklists (or their operational equivalent) than by political, ideological, bureaucratic, and psychological considerations. The Iraq war is a classic instance. For decades to come, scholars will be trying to explain not only how and where the decision to invade Iraq was made but why, in the face of expressed staff misgivings, were we so egregiously unprepared to deal with the consequence of a sweeping military success.[1]

At the theoretical level, we hope (and immodestly believe) that we have closed an important gap in the case against nation building. To date, this case has been based largely on the "argument from history"—the premise that what has regularly happened before will happen again. No doubt history often repeats itself but the proposition that "X" has consistently occurred in the past does not logically warrant the conclusion that it will necessarily happen in the future. In fact, the process appears to be already underway. Barely a month after Iraq's election, and the resulting Shiite "victory," a lengthy story in *The Wall Street Journal* carried the caption "Iraqi Regime May Pose New U.S. Dilemma—Shiite Promoted Policies Concerning Islam, Sunnis Appear Set to Conflict with Washington" (March 3, 2005: A-4).

In utilizing a neo-Darwinian approach to human political behavior, we have added a critical, but previously lacking, explanatory component to the argument against nation building—that is, that authoritarian governments have been the rule (our aforementioned "default option") rather than the exception [in large part] because evolution has endowed our species (just it has the other social primates) with an innate bias toward hierarchical, rather than democratic and egalitarian, social and political structures. That is why democratic governments have been so infrequent in the past and why, even today, they remain a minority among polities; that is why so many "enabling conditions" must be met if a democracy is to be born and survive; that, in short, is why nation building is so often an unpromising enterprise. The case against nation building has previously simply pointed to historical regularities; evolutionary theory provides the missing explanation.

Now for other possible questions about our first resolution. Are not we really suggesting that, for all practical purposes, the United States no longer engage in nation building? Not quite, but almost. We certainly believe that the United States should think not merely twice but several times before trying to export democracy to other countries; further, if we finally decide to make such an attempt, it should be with the full realization that it will be a difficult, uphill struggle.[2] We should also be aware that, if we are successful, the newly created democracy will soon develop "national interests" that may either not coincide with, or may actually work against, our own goals—just as did in the case of Japan and Germany.

We want to make clear that we are speaking here only of nation building. Foreign aid, when essential to save lives threatened by economic disasters, civil wars, or natural catastrophes, as happened to the nations ravaged by the tsunami in early 2005, is quite a different matter. The United States has been traditionally quick to respond and should continue to do so. Quite apart from humanitarian considerations, generosity under these circumstances may work to the advantage both of our own reputation—conceivably offsetting, to some extent, the damage done among Moslem nations in particular and the world community in general by Abu Ghraib—and the international image of democracy itself. But expectations should not run too high. Even the best intentioned actions, as we have repeatedly experienced, are susceptible to misinterpretation.

Our resolution on foreign policy, the reader may have noted, was cast in the future tense: What guidance does it provide for our current nation building efforts in Afghanistan and Iraq? In one sense, not very much. We are now deeply, almost inextricably, committed. Any useful policy proposals would require a better grasp of the political situation in Iraq than we can claim. In strategic terms, however, the basic thrust of the resolution might be quite helpful. The present, oft-proclaimed U.S. intent to establish a "peace-loving democracy" in Iraq[3] carries with it a continuing, perhaps even expanding, commitment of resources and lives over a prolonged period of time. An alternative approach would be to recognize that we have set ourselves a near-impossible (assuredly, in the short-term) task and to rethink our policy in light of that realization. Given the situation in Iraq, one for which we are in some measure responsible, establishing a stable government, let alone a democracy, might be a more realistic objective.

Now for our second "resolution" and our insistence that the democratic cause would be better served if we turned away from nation building and redirected our attention and resources to the social, political, and economic problems that plague us here at home. We identified four of these—a faulty political system; poverty and vast inequalities of income and wealth; the loss of "social capital"; and the failure of our schools to teach democratic citizenship—as especially urgent. Other commentators, equally concerned about the future of the American democracy, might argue and propose a different set of "most worrisome" issues but we would be surprised if one or two of the same items did not appear on almost all lists. In any event, it is less important that we agree on the specific set of problems to be addressed than that we realize the United States faces some serious domestic difficulties—and act accordingly.

This said, we would have to admit the prospects for any concerted corrective measures are pretty bleak. None of the problems we singled out received more than passing mention in the 2004 presidential debates—and then mostly in the context of Senator Kerry's distinction between the interests of the "middle classes" (to whom he was appealing), and those of the "wealthy" (presumably favored by his opponent). Someone whose knowledge of this country was derived solely from listening to, or reading about, the debates, would remain unaware that one-sixth of American families, and an even larger proportion of our children, are officially recognized as living *below* the poverty line, that the proportion has been growing—and that, especially in a democracy, this should be a matter of grave concern.

Nor did a single one of our four major problems appear on President Bush's statement of priorities for his second administration. Nor, to the best of our knowledge, were any of them advanced by the Democrats, nor by any maverick Republican, as competing alternatives to the president's choices. The reform of Social Security, described by skeptics as a solution in search of a problem, is thus likely to be "front and center stage" politically until the 2006 elections. Under these circumstances, it is almost certain that, even if additional resources were made available by a significant reduction in our nation building expenditures, they would not be redirected to "anti-poverty" programs.[4] In fact, we may be headed in the opposite direction: If President Bush's 2005–2006 budget proposals are adopted, there will be a cut in Medicaid,[5] "200,000–300,000 people will lose food stamp benefits" and "a program to help low-income parents will benefit 300,000 fewer children."[6] Under compassionate conservatism we may be moving, as one authority warned a decade ago, toward "a form of societal triage where the system seemingly can provide for the well-being of two-thirds of the populace while sacrificing the remaining third and allowing it to solidify into an underclass."[7]

What, then, is the outlook for our second target, major political reform? Hardly any better. As presently structured, the system demonstrably works nicely for the president; the Republicans, who now comfortably control both the House and Senate, have little reason to push for change; the Democrats have neither the votes nor, until they lose another election or two, the incentive, to raise the issue. Although considerable dissatisfaction has been voiced in a few newspapers and in periodicals aimed at a serious reading public, the subject has not been picked up by the more popular media, and the public at large seems to be essentially unconcerned. The situation may change over the next couple of years, especially if things continue to go badly in Iraq and/or the economy again falters but, at least for the near term, there is little likelihood of anything more than cosmetic change. Now, perhaps even more than ever before, "a shift to a more constructive political competition would require a wrenching alteration of habit, strategy, and worldview by all the participants, at the same time dominant pressures are working against such progress."[8]

The 2004 campaign, with its charges of divisiveness and deliberate dissimulation, on the one hand, and of being irresolute, even unpatriotic, on the other, did not slow the depletion of social capital. In the couple of months between the election and the inauguration, this process was, if anything, accelerated by the questions asked and the answers given during Senate committee hearings held on some of the president's nominees for high office. As one of Britain's leading journals then editorialized, "[P]olitically active Americans are increasingly divided into two well-organized warring tribes who disagree about the most fundamental issues of life."[9] The distrust and ill feelings were not notably lessened by the president's inaugural address and the Democrats' response thereto. The one bright (relatively speaking) spot in the situation was the concern over this widening chasm expressed in recent weeks by some of our leading newspapers and by influential columnists on both sides of the ideological divide. Still, much as we would like to think otherwise, it may be that no change for the better can be expected until many of the leaders of both parties have been replaced—or at least challenged—by the American equivalents of Vaclav Havel and Adam Michnik, who led the restoration of social capital (and eventually the "velvet revolution") in Czechoslovakia.

Dimmest of all, we must concede, are the chances that our public schools will resume the responsibility they once so admirably fulfilled—preparing our young (and literally millions of not so young[10]) for democratic civic participation. There are several reasons for this. Political Correctness (PC), an intellectual ailment now apparently endemic in the United States, frowns upon anything smacking of indoctrination, or of suggesting that one form of government or set of ideas (excepting, of course political correctness) is in any way "better" than another. Persuading our teachers, many ardent advocates of PC, to teach the virtues of democracy might be an even harder task than getting their unions to endorse the idea of merit pay. Little support could be expected from state and local boards of education, some of which seem to be more anxious to ensure that their students are taught that evolution is "only a theory," than that they learn how the American political system functions and the relative virtues and shortcoming of democracy and of other forms of government.

If these were not obstacles enough, there is our federal structure that traditionally has treated education as the province of the states and the resulting difficulty (absent a massive popular groundswell) of shifting this responsibility to the national government or, alternatively, of trying to get 50 states to move in a common direction. And last, of course, there seems to be relatively little public understanding that democracies can function effectively only if their citizens are informed, concerned—and involved.

Now, two brief concluding comments. If we take the president's recent statements at face value, his administration, having apparently learned little from its foray into Iraq, plans to continue and perhaps even expand its nation building efforts. Should this happen, the case against nation building, whether based on history or on neo-Darwinian theory, would clearly have fallen on very, very stony soil. We can only hope, therefore, that future administrations will follow a different policy—and that they do so before whatever is gained (or more likely lost) abroad is greatly overshadowed by the cost and consequences of this policy here at home.

On the domestic front, there is little reason to expect that this administration or this Congress will address the four problems or, in fact, any of the many others we mentioned [although their cumulative effect threatens to undermine the foundations on which our—or any other—democracy rests]. This task, too, will apparently have to await the emergence and accession to power of a new political leadership, one more sensitive to the special needs of democratic polities. Again, we can only hope that this occurs before irreparable damage is done to our own.

Here, too, an evolutionary perspective may be relevant, if not necessarily consoling. No species, whether plant or animal, is guaranteed immortality; they survive if they can adapt to the challenges presented by a changing environment, they become extinct if they cannot. Much the same, as many philosophers and historians have stressed, is true of cultures, civilizations—and governments.[11] As Arthur Schlesinger has reminded us, "The world got along without democracy until two centuries ago . . ." (2004: 16). Unless we are wiser and luckier than our predecessor democratic regimes, the world may again be compelled to do so in the not too-distant future.[12]

Notes

Chapter One   Introduction

1. In American political discourse, the term "nation building" has come to mean building *democratic* nations.

2. An equally obvious but perhaps less important question is—Given our repeated failures, why have Democratic and Republican administrations alike not only persisted in but, as in Iraq and Afghanistan, expanded our nation building efforts? For this, social scientists have advanced a number of reasons. There is the apparently unshakable American conviction that all problems are solvable if only we try harder and throw enough money at them (prohibition and the "war against drugs" are classic examples). Although not unique in this respect, our political parties and politicians find it remarkably difficult to admit that they have been wrong, In one of his "Fireside Chats," President Franklin D. Roosevelt declared that "the country needs . . . bold, persistent experimentation. It is commonsense to take a method and try it; if it fails, admit it frankly, and try another." As James Chace, with perhaps a specific incumbent in mind, tartly remarks, "No national politician could talk like that today" (2004: 17).

    Nor should we forget that we are notoriously a nation of do-gooders: most of us believe that the American democracy "with its individual freedom, popular democracy, and market economics is also the best design for all humanity" and that we have almost a moral obligation to extend its blessing and benefits to less fortunate nations. There could hardly be a better example of this than President Woodrow Wilson's declaration on Armistice Day, "It will now be our fortunate duty to assist by example, by sober, friendly counsel, and by material aid in the establishment of just democracy throughout the world" (Teachout, 2003: 153). Rudyard Kipling himself could not have put it more clearly. From this perspective, it was not too difficult to view the events of "9/11" as providing an opportunity, to quote the then secretary of defense, "to refashion the world" (both Wilson and Rumsfeld are cited by Urquhart (2003: 10).

    Furthermore, there often soon develop influential public bureaucracies and private enterprises that have a vested interest in nation building. For example, barely a year after Iraq fell, almost 90 billion dollars was earmarked for "reconstruction" there; two years after the occupation of Afghanistan, the amount requested for this country was just short of 30 billion dollars. A reasonably plausible case can be made, moreover, that the United States itself gains, directly or indirectly, from the establishment of sister democratic systems (on the so-called democratic peace, see Dixon, 1994; Russett, 1993; Russett and Antholis, 1992).

3. For more on the SSSM and its implications for public policy than most readers probably want to know, see Somit and Peterson (2003).

4. For a full statement of this contention, see the aforementioned Somit and Peterson (1997).

5. How to designate this capability? In an earlier work, we used the cumbersome but most commonly accepted term—"indoctrinability." The best substitute that comes to mind, though it has a slightly different connotation, is "credulity."

6. Once launched, Daniel Bell emphasized in an excellent but surely mis-titled study, "[ideologies] take on life of their own. A truly powerful ideology opens a new vision of life . . . it remains part of the moral repertoire to be drawn upon by intellectuals, theologians, or moralists. . . . Unlike economies or outmoded technologies, they do not disappear . . . they can be called upon and reformulated throughout the history of a civilization" (1961: 60–61).

7. As those who are familiar with the history of political ideas know that, until the 1800s, philosophical thought and public opinion alike favored authoritarian, and enthusiastically decried democratic, political doctrines.

8. Dennett (1995: 516); Pinker (2002: 2). Summarizing a number of recent public opinion studies, Allen MacNeill (2004) reported that "1) The vast majority of the American public (83–90%, college educated or not) are creationists at some level; 2) Only among American scientists . . . does belief in a non-guided evolution exceed a bare majority (55%); and 3) Even among American scientists, belief in what could only be called 'intelligent design' is close to half (45%)." Indeed, the United States features less acceptance of Darwinian theory than most other nations. Polls in 1991 and 1993 showed that only about 35 percent of Americans accepted evolutionary theory as an explanation for human behavior (Stonjek, 2004). In January 2004, Georgia's school superintendent proposed the omission of reference to "evolution" in guidelines for teaching middle- and high-school science. This subject was also absent from the guidelines in Ohio, West Virginia, New Mexico, Alabama, and Pennsylvania (*San Diego Union Tribune*, January 30, 2004: A-7). Little seems to have changed in the quarter-century since Richard Alexander lamented that "humans have not only failed throughout history to acquire an understanding that they have evolved to maximize reproduction, but that even today they deny the possibility vehemently. . . . We can still marvel at the hostility it engenders" (cited in Lockard and Paulus, 1988: 136–137; and see Mazur, 2005).

9. On this long-standing issue, we should note, only a tentative conclusion is as yet warranted. Primatology is a relatively recent discipline and has experienced drastic revisions in its view of primate nature as new research findings have been reported, the Bonobo studies being the most recent example. This said, the portrait of political man that has so far emerged suggests that Hobbes's unflattering delineation may come considerably closer to the mark than Locke's or Rousseau's.

10. Celibacy, monogamy, willingness to give up one's life for "flag and country," or for a political ideology or religious belief are among the examples that come immediately to mind.

11. We undertook a similar census almost a decade ago and are using the same chapter title to report the new findings.

12. And, to a lesser extent, the other members of the coalition.

Chapter Two Authoritarian Government: The Default Option

1. For a good, brief introduction to evolutionary theory, see Mayr (2001).
2. For more contemporary applications in evolutionary psychology, see Barkow, Cosmides, and Tooby (1993); Barrett, Dunbar, and Lycett (2002); Buss (1999).
3. "An animal may be said to be dominant if it has a high probability of winning hostile encounters" (Moyer, 1987: 2). For various approaches to dominance, see Bernstein (1981, 2004); Jolly (1985); Walters and Seyfarth (1987).
4. As with many other aspects of behavior in the natural world, this represents something of an oversimplification. See, e.g., Stanford (2001).
5. This is also the pattern with macaques (Bernstein, 1981; Eaton, 1976; Koford, 1963) and baboons (Hausfater, Altmann, and Altmann, 1982; Watanabe and Smuts, 2004). There is, so far, little evidence of this among gorillas (Stewart and Harcourt, 1987).
6. In Robert Frank's succinct phrase, "[T]he physical characteristics and even the behavior of a species evolve in such ways as to give individual members of the species the greatest reproductive advantage" (1985: 132). For earlier classic expositions of neo-Darwinism, see Simpson (1944, 1953) and Mayr (1970). See also Maynard-Smith (1982) and Dawkins (1989).
7. However, some questions on this have recently been raised by Ellis (1995).
8. To complicate matters, one animal may be subordinate to another with respect to one resource, such as food, and dominant over this same animal with respect to another resource, such as a preferred sleeping area (Jolly, 1985). Some contend that dominance should not be defined in terms of access to resources but rather as "approach–withdrawal" behavior (Walters and Seyfarth, 1987). In addition, coalitions can develop where relatively low-ranking males, by working with others, may do well. For an excellent example of this among savanna baboons, see Hall and DeVore (1965) for the story of old Kovu, low-ranking in dyadic dominance relations but near the top of the hierarchy because of his association with more powerful allies. And see Watanabe and Smuts (2004).
9. Until quite recently, orthodox neo-Darwinian theory held that natural selection and, consequently, evolution operated purely at the *individual* and not at the group or species level. For changing opinions on this issue, see Wilson and Sober (1994) and Wilson (1995).
10. Interestingly enough, rhesus monkeys will give up perks that they have gained in order to view pictures of dominant leaders in their troop (Chase, 2005).
11. For arguments from a biological perspective that march in a different direction from ours, see Rubin (2002); Boehm (2004).
12. Some have argued that the tendency toward hierarchy and despotism in humans has only increased as society has become more complex. See Summers (2005).
13. "In a way, it's not surprising that the rediscovery of human nature has taken us so long. Being everywhere we look, it tends to elude us" (Wright, 1994: 8).
14. Many educated people try to explain this phenomenon in terms of culture. As Dunbar (2005: 961) says, "I continue to be surprised by the number of educated people (many of them biologists) who think that offering explanations for human behavior in terms of culture somehow disproves the suggestion that human behavior can be explained in Darwinian evolutionary terms."

15. For a detailed exposition of this view by the best known of contemporary ethologists, see Eibl-Eibesfeldt (1989).

16. Ridley (1994: 119) reduced the proposition to a single sentence "Humans are a highly social species whose society is nearly always stratified in some way."

17. However, note Myers's comment, "No regime ever needed to subject its citizens to a lifetime of brainwashing in order to make them follow their natural inclinations" (Myers, 2004: 138).

18. On a related point, Henrich and Boyd (1998) suggest that humans are programmed to "conform" to general expectations.

19. Essentially paraphrasing Easton (1965), a government (or regime or political community) is "legitimate" when a population believes that, on balance, it meets its needs and interests and reflects its cultural and/or ethnic identity. When governments (regimes, etc.) are no longer perceived as legitimate, they can still extract obedience by force and threat but in most instances their days are numbered.

20. For one interesting application, see Meyer-Emerick (2004).

21. For a masterful overview of the rise, decline, and subsequent resurrection of Darwinism as applied to *human* behavior, see Carl Degler's *In Search of Human Nature* (1991).

22. See, e.g., Ervin Staub (1989), and Herman C. Kelman and V. Lee Hamilton (1989). Barrington Moore is curiously ambivalent. Moore (1978: 7) agrees that "moral codes, moral anger, and hence a sense of social injustice may have some very important roots in human biology" but apparently does not recognize the possibility that "obedience" may also have a biological basis.

23. A key element in neo-Darwinian thought, we should add, is that this is a false dichotomy and that the two are nigh inseparable in the actual development of an organism's behavior.

24. We have relied heavily upon Miller (1986) and Kelman and Hamilton (1989) for a description of the Milgram experiments.

25. Apparently unaware of Milgram's work, C.K. Hoffing and his colleagues (1966) carried out a "real life" experiment in which nurses in a hospital were instructed by a "physician" to administer a certain drug to one of their patients. The instructions violated several hospital regulations—and the "physician" issuing the instruction (via phone) was not known to the nurse. Of 22 nurses so ordered, 21 were prepared to obey.

    Rank and Jacobson (1977) achieved quite different results in a somewhat similar inquiry but, as Miller (1986: 85–86) points out, there were important structural differences between the two studies.

26. With only isolated pockets of quasi-democratic governments as in Renaissance Italy, and so on.

27. For recent opinion on this matter, see McGrew (1991).

28. "Belief of this kind has two essential prerequisites. First, a high level of language competence. . . . Secondly, a conscious high level use of explanation based on causal theory, i.e., the belief that one event causes another. . . . Both these requirements and particularly their combination make it unlikely that we shall find belief in this form in non-human species" (Premack, 1988: 174). Darwin himself, as Wright (1994: 185) remarks, had suggested that the word "moral" be reserved to *Homo sapiens* alone.

29. As the Gnostic "Gospel of Philip" puts it, "That is the way it is in the world—human beings make gods, and worship their creation" (Pagels, 1979: 122). See also Peterson (2002, in press).

Chapter Three   What is a Democracy?: Toward a Working Definition

1. For example, see Dahl, Shapiro, and Cheibub (2003).
2. For instance, see Bachrach (1967).
3. One current subspecies of the participatory democratic school of thought is associated with the work of German philosopher Jurgen Habermas, who calls for a sociopolitical system that would be based on dialogic communication and open discourse. He contends that the late capitalist system suffers a legitimation crisis and that transformation of the system looms. New norms are needed. How will these develop? Habermas (1975: 89) answers

   > Only communication ethics guarantees the generality of admissible norms and the autonomy of acting subjects solely through the discursive redeemability of the validity claims with which norms appear. That is, generality is guaranteed in that the only norms that may claim generality are those on which everyone affected agrees (or would agree) without constraint if they enter into (or were to enter into) a process of discursive will-formation.

   Habermas has authored a series of works laying out his theory of communicative action in much more detail (Habermas, 1979, 1984). He argues that citizens will test the validity claims of the various ideas and norms under debate. According to his final analysis (1975: 105), "The validity claim of norms is grounded not in the irrational volitional acts of the contracting parties, but in the rationally motivated recognition of norms, which may be questioned at any time." And what determines which validity claim is best? Habermas claims that the better argument that emerges from a cooperative dialogue should rule—if a consensus forms around this one possibility. The political community, through dialogue, will determine which norms will guide discourse, debate, and decision-making; this is the essence of "communicative rationality." His theory of communication assumes that there is no universal truth to guide the shaping of the norms agreed upon by a people. Development and emergence of such norms must be a result of debate and discussion producing consensus.

   John Dryzek (1990) argues that the wedding of communicative rationality and democracy can alleviate many of the problems faced by democratic polities in the twentieth century. Arrangements to assist in what Dryzek calls "discursive democracy," would include open public spheres for debate, emphasizing active citizenship and vibrant public discourse. Institutions that nurture discursive democracy will protect people from the power of self-interested groups and from technocrats/bureaucrats asserting their technical expertise as a source of power. The end result will be a more genuine democracy (see Gutmann and Thompson, 1996).

4. Postmodern democratic theory also emphasizes the individual and the minority (see Mara, 2003). For instance, the Other is an important theme among postmodern philosophers. Stephen White (1991: 19) has noted that "Other is always pushed aside, marginalized, forcibly homogenized and devalued . . ."

Rational ideals of the modern era have it that we must try to explain all things, that there are underlying explanations to account for everything. We try to make "Same" explain all components of a particular arena in common terms—including individuals and groups. We want the American "melting pot" to take people from different backgrounds and somehow make them "American"; in that sense, we try to make Other (people from different backgrounds) into "Same" (becoming good Americans, adopting American ideals and values). By trying to reduce everything to Same, we are repressing Other.

There is a striking political metaphor here, according to Bernstein (and see Critchley, 1992). Bernstein (1992: 71) claims,

> For the "logic" at work here is the "logic" at work in cultural, political, social, and economic imperialism and colonization—even the "logic" of ethical imperialism where the language of reciprocal recognition and recon- ciliation masks the violent reduction of . . . "the Other" . . . to "more of the same."

For the postmodern analyst, the suppression of the "Other" is a form of vio- lence. What is needed is a "letting be." The late Jacques Derrida, a major post- modern figure, calls out for "the respect for the other as what it is: other. Without this acknowledgment, which is not a knowledge, or let us say without this 'letting be' of an existent (Other) as something existing outside me in the essence of what is . . . , no ethics would be possible" (quoted in Bernstein, 1992: 184–185). And Derrida clearly wants an ethics of tolerance and "letting be." We must never cease questioning; we must not allow one truth to become dominant and, thus, to disallow other truths to coexist.

Again, to emphasize the political relevance of such ideas, consider Bernstein's (1993: 106) comments—

> Now although Derrida has not developed a well-articulated political theory, he is extremely incisive in exposing those tendencies in "the history of the West" which suppress and repress difference . . . , and otherness. He exposes the hidden violence of marginalization and exclusion. This is why I think Derrida is so relevant for all those who have suffered from discrimination, oppression, and exclusion. The task for democratic theory today is to think through how to do justice to both universality and particularity, sameness and difference, to conceive and develop practices in which we recognize the indeterminableness of conflict and nevertheless can learn to respect the otherness of the other.

The postmodern thinker would argue that democracy is only possible if we resist the temptation to marginalize/suppress/oppress/repress Other. That is, a "letting be" and tolerance of Other/different is mandated if we are truly to expe- rience freedom in a democracy. Here, the emphasis is on the freedom of the minority (Other), the commitment to preventing their claims/understand- ings/values being suppressed. There is not much extant postmodern work speci- fying the institutional features that would characterize a postmodern democratic society (for one effort to be more explicit, see Mouffe, 1993, 2000). However, we do see an emphasis on protection of minority rights, civil and political liberties, that which we term the "rule of law." Although there are many critics of the postmodern perspective, it does add its own flavor to the debate over the nature of democracy—with an emphasis on protecting Other (rights of minorities and those with different perspectives than the dominant views in a society).

5. Whether at regularly prescribed intervals as in the United States or within a certain period of time as in England.
6. Dahl stresses that we must take into account preelection, election, and interelection institutions if we are to affirm the existence of polyarchy; see Dahl (1956).
7. See http://www.sv.ntnu.no/iss/data/Vanhanen.
8. For members of the 2003 survey, see Karatynycky, Piano, and Puddington (2003: 305).
9. For the actual ratings on a country-by-country basis, see http://www.cidcm. umd.edu/inscr/polity/index.htm.
10. We limit our discussion here to *representative* democracy since this has been the form of all democracies *at the national level* since Athenian days.
11. Casper and Tufis (2002) find that party fractionalization, one index of party competition, is highly correlated with the three measures of democracy noted earlier.

Chapter Four   Democratic Nation Building: From Concept to Operational "Checklist"

1. Here, we might note that it is not at all clear that free markets necessarily go with democracy. For a case study of Russia, see Higgins (2004).
2. See a review of this by Vidal (2003).
3. Dobbins et al. (2003: chapter 9).
4. As another commentator (Cordesman, 2004: 67) notes, "The United States should once again start thinking in terms of decades." And note Cabe's comment that "the commitment to Afghanistan may have to last as much as a decade . . ." (2002: 6). An article in the *Economist* echoes these sentiments ("Manifest Destiny Warmed Up?" 2004: 21): "If the peace is to endure, if the rule of law is to be established, if democratic institutions are to take root, you had better be prepared for a lengthy undertaking, with men, money, and limitless patience."
5. Cordesman makes much the same point. For instance, with respect to Afghanistan, he (2004: 65) says that

   the United States (and a number of its allies) are repeating many of the nation-building mistakes of Iraq in a country with far fewer resources and far less hope. The security effort is marginal and carried out on the cheap, and each incremental security fix lags behind the growth of the problem.

6. This is consistent, of course, with Fukuyama's argument that there is a two-stage process in democratic nation building.
7. Others have also spoken of the danger of depending on economic liberalism to produce robust democracy in formerly nondemocratic states. See, e.g., DiJohn (2005), Sanin (2005), Wade (2005).
8. Even at that, some conservative/libertarian scholars think that nation building is folly (See, e.g., Dempsey, 2001, 2002). Rosett (2004: 2) notes the following in a *Wall Street Journal* opinion piece: "The liberal minds Mr. Clinton exemplified

turns on the idea that those in power can somehow reengineer the nature of mankind." Ironically, she (2004: 2) writes in praise of President Bush's statement issued just after 9/11: "We're not into nation-building."

9. The following discussion is based on Dobbins et al. (2003); Pei and Kasper (2003); Jennings (2003).
10. See, e.g., Karatynycky, Piano, and Puddington (2003).
11. See, inter alia, Dobbins et al. (2003); Pei and Kasper (2003).
12. And we should not forget an even earlier unsuccessful American intervention in Haiti from 1915 to 1934.
13. For other recent and largely dismal analyses, see Bandow (2004); Kamber, (2005); "Whose Coup in Haiti" (2004).

Chapter Five   Democracy: The Requisite "Enabling Conditions"—No Small Order

1. No, not Herculean; Hercules was successful in his labors.
2. Leonard Wantchekon has recently contented that "based on recent, empirical evidence of post-civil war democratization in El Salvador, Mozambique, and elsewhere, I show that democracy can arise directly from anarchy" (2004: 17). This contention rests, to be sure, on a rather elastic use of the terms "anarchy" and, as the countries mentioned might hint, "democracy."
3. For a discussion of these and related aspects of civil war issues, see Lomborg (2004).
4. From Plato on, philosophers have debated the ideal "size" (i.e., population) of governments in general and of democracies in particular. For a recent review of this literature, see Alesina and Spolare (2004).
5. See Casper (2001); Casper and Tufis (2002); Lipset (1963); Muller (1988); Muller and Seligson (1994); Przeworski et al. (2001); Vanhanen (1984).
6. "[M]alnourished children may receive less education because they are not seen as good 'investments' " (*The Economist*, May 8, 2004: 74).
7. According to *The Economist* (April 24, 2004: 6) the UN report also "found that most Latin Americans supported the return of 'authoritarian' governments in place of democratic ones. Corruption, inequality and poor economic growth are to blame."
8. Apparently proceeding on the maxim "if you don't succeed at first, try, try again," a senior department of defense official has proposed that the military establish a major organization of "System Administrators" that "would focus on bringing dysfunctional states into the mainstream through the type of nation building operations seen in Iraq, the Balkans, and Eastern Africa" (Jaffe, 2004: 1). Given our track record in these areas, this is obviously just what we need. For a book-length exposition of the idea, see Barnett (2004).
9. See Casper (2001); Casper and Tufis (2002); Deutsch (1961); McCrone and Cnudde (1967); Banks (1972); Vanhanen (1984).
10. Harold Lasswell is usually credited with popularizing these two terms in the 1930s, although the underlying concepts date back at least to Mosca and Pareto. The somewhat broader term "influentials" came into wide usage a couple of decades later but seems lately to have been replaced by the not altogether flattering designation "chattering class."

11. For a litany of U.S. blunders on almost all of these matters in Iraq, see Peter Galbraith, (2004: 42–46).

12. "Democracy requires that losers of elections believe they will not lose their essential values or their lives. Such trust and confidence takes decades to develop. It is Utopian to believe otherwise." (Gelb, 2004: A-12).

13. Some readers may remember the last sentence of Philip Roth's *Portnoy's Complaint* where, after listening silently to Portnoy for the entire book, the psychiatrist speaks—"Und now ve go to work."

14. "Until [Thomas] Paine tried to salvage it, the term 'democracy' had been deployed only as an insult" (Hitchens, 2004: 134).

15. "Let her and Falsehood grapple; who ever knew Truth put to the worse, in a free and open encounter?"

16. Thus, President George W. Bush said, in September 2003, "Most important of all, Iraqis are on the road to democratic self-government" (*Wall Street Journal*, September 19, 2003: A-10). And, perhaps more excusably, President Woodrow Wilson on Armistice Day, 1919—"It will now be our fortunate duty to assist by example, by sober, friendly counsel, and by material aid in the establishment of just democracy throughout the world" (Teachout, 2003: 153).

17. Prime Minister Lloyd George warmly congratulated the then Colonial Secretary Winston Churchill, who was assigned the post–World War I task of managing the British-controlled former Turkish territories for making a new nation—Iraq—out of a "mere collection of tribes" (Karl, 2004: D-10).

18. For a neo-Darwinian explanation of ethnic conflict, see Thayer (2004). For a similar approach to religion, see D. S. Wilson (2002).

19. "The town of Zvornik in Serb-held Bosnia once had a dozen mosques. The 1991 census listed 60% of the residents as Muslim Slavs. By the end of the war, the town was 100% Serb. Brank Grujic, the Serb-appointed mayor, informed us: 'There never were any mosques in Zvornik.' No doubt he did not believe it. He knew that there had been mosques in Zvornik. But his children and grand-children would come to be taught the lie. Serb leaders would turn it into accepted historical fact" (Urquhart, 2003: 11–12).

20. We should not forget, though, that even long-standing religious differences may eventually soften to permit the emergence of a democratic polity, as evidenced by Switzerland, Belgium, Germany, and Austria—to mention only some of the better-known instances. But we should also not forget, first, that all of these are developed countries enjoying the requisite conditions discussed above and, sec-ond, that in all of them democracies took literally decades to develop.

21. See, for thoroughly disheartening reading, Levene and Roberts (1999); Bartov and Mack (2002); Deak (2002); and Fox (2004), as well as the literature cited in note 26 below. Except in one or two instances, the developed nations, including the United States, have done little, individually or collectively, other than to issue the usual statements of disapproval in such cases, e.g., as Rwanda, Sudan, East Timor, and for some time in Bosnia before the intervention.

22. For a contrary view, see Rauf (2004); for a thoughtful review essay, see Geertz (2003). See also Gerecht (2004); Kepel (2004); Buruma and Margalit (2004).

23. There is some disagreement among different commentators on the numbers. According to the *Wall Street Journal* (June 22, 2004, A-1), Freedom House says there are 47 democracies—not the 56 given by the *Economist*. Another source

(*This Week*, June 25, 2004: 8) reports that there are 57 member states in the Organization of the Islamic Conference.

24. However reasonable, this is manifestly not the timetable projected by those setting U.S. policy.

25. See Gill (2002) for a discussion of the role of ethnic rivalry in shaping the politics of 26 ex-Communist states up to 2000.

26. For those with strong stomachs, see Chua (2003); Kaufman (2002); Naimark (2001); Deak (2002).

27. Vladimir Gilgorov, cited by Samantha Power (2004: 35). But this is hardly new. After the Hapsburg and Romanov dynasties collapsed in 1918, "[A] flurry of new states emerged and the first thing they did was to set about privileging their national 'ethnic' majority—defined by language, religion, or antiquity, or all three—at the expense of inconvenient local minorities, who were consigned to second-class status, permanent resident strangers in their own home" (Judt, 2003: 8).

28. This could obviously be refined into an ordinal scale.

29. In the most unpromising places, with expectations of almost immediate successful results.

Chapter Six   Will the Real Democracies Please Stand Up?

1. Granted, no amount of data can establish that "what has been" will necessarily continue to be the case. Still it is not unreasonable to suggest that such well-established patterns are like to persist for some time into the future.

2. A few Italian Renaissance city-states, such as Florence, could possibly be added to the list. Dahl notes that, ca. 1100, popular rule began to manifest itself in halting steps in Italy. However, these were small-scale polities, encompassing both small areas and small populations. Furthermore, these so-called republics were mixed in nature, with the "people" being only one of several constituent groups involved in governance (see, for instance, Held, 1993). A book, edited by R. W. Davis, outlines the origins of modern free states in the West—and indicates the problems with confidently saying that, for instance, Italian city-state republics actually were democracies (Davis, 1995). And, by the 1300s, decline began to set in, for a variety of reasons. Dahl (1998: 16) observes that the enemies of Italian republicanism included "economic decline, corruption, oligarchy, war, conquest, and seizure of power by authoritarian rulers."

Other harbingers of contemporary democracy? The Vikings featured local assemblies from 600 to 1000. Regional assemblies developed in Scandinavia later, from 930 on. The first meaningful English parliaments met in the medieval era, from 1272 to 1307 (under Edward I) (see Dahl, 1998: chapter 2).

3. See the chapter entitled "Will the Real Democracies Please Stand Up" in Somit and Peterson (1997: 31–47). And it can certainly be argued that Athens was a bit shaky on the "rule of law" (see, for instance, Schwartzberg, 2004).

4. Robert Dahl (1971, 1991), with whom we are inclined to agree, is notably less ready than Vanhanen to grant that designation.

5. We discussed these data sources in chapter 3.

6. For an excellent analysis of the resulting difficulties, see Munck and Verkullen (2002). In addition, we must note that there are numerous "one-off" ratings on

such overlapping matters as that of repressive regimes, listing the "worst of the worst" and the "best of the worst" (*Atlantic Monthly*, 2004: 52–53), of economic freedom (Miles et al., 2005); of social progress (Estes, 2004); and, to take a last example, of freedom of the press—with the United States in thirty-first place (Reporters Without Borders, October 2003).

7. See chapter 3 for greater detail.

8. We do not think that even the most generous of the typically "glass is full" Freedom House analysts would argue that people who are only "Partially Free" are likely to have a democratic government.

9. July 10–16, 2004.

10. As the transformation of Germany barely a year after Hitler came to power. Nor are older, long-established democracies immune. Consider the reduction of civil liberties that has occurred in the United States since 9/11.

11. And see the discussion by Diamond (2001).

12. Part free countries, as rated by Freedom House, are *not* counted as democracies.

13. Despite the salubrious trends, one ought always to recall that during and after World War I, the largest portion of the 29 European governments had some sort of representative government. However, matters can change quickly in the world of politics. As Ferguson (2005: A-10) notes, "Unfortunately, it didn't last. Six had become dictatorships by 1925, a further four by 1930, six by 1935 and eight by 1940."

14. And see Gill (2002) for a detailed discussion of political change up until 2000 in the post–Soviet Union era.

Chapter Seven American Nation Building, 1945–2005: Costs and Consequences

1. According to Marx (1978: 594), in his *The Eighteenth Brumaire of Louis Bonaparte*, "Hegel remarks somewhere that all great, world-historical facts occur, as it were, twice. He has forgotten to add: the first time as tragedy, the second as farce." In this instance, there was little that was farcical.

2. By the 1950s, mainland China and North Korea were added to the list of suspect nations.

3. Critics, of course, alleged a less laudable agenda—the use of foreign aid primarily to further American business interests.

4. A susceptibility satirized, as some of our readers may recall, in the film *The Mouse That Roared*.

5. *Congressional Quarterly* (December 17, 1994: 3568). Challenging this calculation, Senator Jesse Helms put the price at twice this amount. Neither estimate includes, we should add, the cost of the Korean and Vietnam wars.

6. Two photographs will probably never be forgotten by those who saw them. One was of a senior South Vietnamese officer executing a North Vietnamese captive; the other, of a naked little Vietnamese girl, screaming with fear, running down the road after a U.S. air attack.

7. Some authorities contend that public faith and confidence in government institutions has also eroded in other Western democracies and that most of them are "troubled" (Dalton, 2002; Pharr, Putnam, and Dalton, 2001: 295).

8. "The trials and tribulations of the American republic have a way of setting the agenda for other democratic societies—for better or for worse" (Elshtain, 1995: 1).

9. As of early 2005, according to a UN report, Kosovo had made "insufficient progress" toward meeting international standards with regard to human rights, respect for minorities, and law and order, that it was "premature to consider settling its long-term status . . ." (*The Economist*, February 19, 2005: 6).

10. See, ironically, Donald Rumsfeld's passionate brief against a nation building policy in Iraq (Rumsfeld, 2003).

11. One of the most frequently voiced theories views Vice President Cheney as the major influence in this apparent change of heart. For example—"Cheney had barely moved into the vice president's office when he started planning for the removal of Saddam Hussein . . ." (*This Week*, September 2, 2004: 18).

12. There has also been some speculation that Syria may be the next country targeted for regime change; if so, this creates the intriguing possibility of a presidential epiphany on the road to Damascus.

13. But this was only the beginning. According to Senator Kerry—admittedly not altogether an objective observer—by mid-September 2004, the Bush administration had some 23 different reasons for invading Iraq.

14. A recurring criticism (voiced by some of our own journalists) is that American reporters, "embedded" in a military unit, too often take on the values, attitudes, and perspectives of the troops with whom they live day in and day out.

15. *New York Times* News Service, published in *San Diego Union Tribune* (September 21, 2004: A-2).

16. *The Economist*, November 27, 2004: 78.

17. *The Economist, Pocket World in Figures* (2004: 237).

18. "Iraq Body Count" (2005).

19. For instance, some 800 Iraqi civilians, police, army, and national guard personnel were murdered because of their association with either the interim Iraqi government or the occupying forces (*The Economist*, January 21, 2005: 32).

20. At Najaf, "some two thousand insurgents and hundreds of civilians [were killed] before a deal was finally brokered"; at Falluja, the decision to send in the Marines "resulted in thousands of deaths" (Anderson, 2005: 59).

21. *Cursor Magazine*, http://www.cursor.org/stories/civiliandeaths.htm.

22. Though perhaps less so, especially for women, in some rural areas of Afghanistan.

23. In terms of "human development" (which subsumes, inter alia, education, health, life expectancy, gender equality, poverty—and hope) it ranks 173rd out of 178 nations (UN Development Programme, 2005).

24. As of the end of 2004, we had "only" 18,000 soldiers, and were spending "only" about $10 billion annually, in Afghanistan (*The Economist*, December 4, 2004: 44).

25. "On ground in Iraq, Capt. Ayers writes his own playbook" (*Wall Street Journal*, September 22, 2004: A-1, A-16). The senior military saw the situation somewhat differently—"With Vietnam winding down, the services were turning their focus back to the Cold War requirements of defending Europe. Because this was also a time of tough budgets, military value was being measured primarily by the capability of the services to meet that commitment and only that commitment" (Clancy, 2004: 141). Bruce Hoffman notes that "the United States is the latest victim in a problem that has long afflicted the world's governments and

militaries when they are confronted with insurgencies: namely, a striking inability to absorb and apply the lessons learned in previous counterinsurgency campaigns" (2004: 42). For an on-the-ground description, see Kaplan (2004).

26. As the Russians also discovered in Chechnya and, earlier, Afghanistan.

27. www.antiwar.com/casualty.

28. Of course, we did not fight the war unaided, nor did our allies escape unscathed, in terms of killed and wounded. But our concern in this book is with the pros and cons of *American* policy.

29. One thinks wistfully of an era when Senator Dirksen could become famous by remarking that "a few million here, a few million there, and pretty soon you're talking real money."

30. We rely here on the figures in *The New York Times*, "Safety second," (August 8, 2004, WK-11). The *Times* then compares these expenditures with "a Pentagon estimate that containing [i.e., rather than deposing] Saddam Hussein would have cost roughly $2.5 billion a year . . ."

31. Defense Secretary Donald Rumsfeld originally estimated the cost of invading Iraq at $50 billion; Deputy Defense Secretary Paul Wolfowitz thought that "Iraq oil revenue of $50 to $100 billion, instead of U.S. taxpayer dollars, would pay for the occupation and reconstruction." White House Economic Adviser Lawrence Lindsay, who estimated the cost to be between $100 and $200 billion, resigned three months later. *Reason on Line*, February 16, 2005, http://.reason.com/had/cp 021605shtml.

32. a255.g.akamaitech.net/7/255/2422/23feb20050900/www.gpoaccess.gov/usbudget/fy06/pdf/hist.pdf.

33. The following gives some sense of the speed with which the administration reversed the policy of its predecessor: "In January 2001 the Congressional Budget Office projected surpluses averaging 4.5 percent of national income over the ten year span 2002–2011. [On October, 2004] the CBO projected deficits averaging 2.3 percent of the national income over the same ten-year span" (Diane Johnson, 2004: 28).

34. A Council on Foreign Relations survey in late 2004 found that only 14% of their respondents felt that "bringing democratic government to other nations should be a "very important" objective of American foreign policy" (*The Economist*, "Do they love us?" October 2, 2004: 33).

35. Kevin Phillips captured the essence of this belief when he wrote that "from the White House to Capitol Hill, a critical weakness in American politics and governance is becoming woefully apparent—the frightening inability of the nation's leaders to face . . . the unprecedented problems and opportunities facing the country" (1990: ix). For recent expressions of this concern, to offer only a very small cross-section of an abundant literature, see Dahl (2001); Crenson and Ginsberg (2002); Patterson (2002); and Skocpol (2004).

36. For a not altogether unbiased commentary, see Byrd (2004)

37. Also perhaps less than strictly objective, Brzezinski, 2004; Clarke, 2004; Goldberg, Goldberg, and Greenwald, 2002; Greenstein, 2003; Lapham, 2004.

38. As the story read, the number of those without health insurance was "up 4 million since our compassionate conservative president came to power" (*The Week*, September 17, 2004: 18).

39. For recent studies, see Iceland (2003), Shipler (2004).

40. *Wall Street Journal* (August 8–27, 2004: A-1, A-4).
41. In all fairness, we do not seem to treat our American impoverished any worse than we treat those in other countries. Among the 21 "rich nations" covered in the study, we were in a 4-way tie for seventh place—"When it comes to direct [foreign] aid, the United States is far stingier, coming in nineteenth on the index, ahead of only Greece and New Zealand" (*The Atlantic Monthly*, "Ranking the rich," September 2004: 48, citing "Ranking the Rich: the 2004 Commitment to Development Index," Center for Global Development/Foreign Policy). For a comparative analysis, see Alesina and Glaesar (2004).
42. Cited in *This Week* (February 11, 2005: 18).
43. George Modelski (1988: 11) puts it nicely:

> How does all of this bear on the prospects for the United States? If we are right about the strength of the process of democratization and the composition of the agenda of global problems then it is also evident that among the likely alternatives the United States is probably the best equipped for forwarding that process and that agenda. Within a democratic community emerging on the basis of a zone of peace, it could serve as a headquarters, the largest and most active workshop of political practice, in itself a microcosm of world society. Where but in the United states do all segments of the human race live in reasonable harmony, in a working model of how the world's peoples might coexist? A united Europe could conceivably serve such a purpose but Europe is not yet united and might take some time achieving that condition. It seems harder, on the other hand, to think of Japan, or China, serving as laboratories for democratic experiments. How else, in the end, can the diversity of world cultures be integrated into one world system than by means of democratic practices?

44. *The Economist*, September 25 (2004: 96–97).
45. For a sobering analysis, see Kotikoff and Burns (2004).
46. Two months before the 2004 presidential election, a leading British journal asked—"Why does barely half of the eligible [American] electorate bother to vote? Why are so many people banned from voting? Why is this election awash with corporate money and dominated by negative campaigning . . . ? Why are so many congressional districts such a very peculiar shape?" The article also called attention, among other aspects needing improvement, to the "all-or-none" nature of the electoral college, and the fact that "no more than 30 seats of the 435 in the House of Representatives are competitive" (*The Economist*, "No way to run a democracy," September 18, 2004: 13).
47. One irony is that while there is severe partisan division at the elite level, the citizenry at large is not fractured politically and is, in the main, moderate (Fiorina, 2005; Stimson, 2004).
48. As the reader may recall, the Supreme Court ruled in the prisoners' behalf—two years later.
49. In a mid-2003 poll covering 19 countries, 37% of the respondents, and a majority of those in 13 countries, saw the United States as having a negative influence on world affairs (PIPA, June 4, 2003).
50. Only 32% of those polled in Great Britain supported the Iraq war (*The Economist*, October 2, 2004: 55). As Stanley Hoffman wrote, America's "friends

and allied [were] shocked by Washington's unilateralism and repudiation of international obligations" (*New York Review*, 2004: 7).

51. For example, see Greenberg and Dratel (2005).

52. See J.R. Schlesinger (2004), Ray (2004), Rose (2004), Hersh (2004).

53. A Gallup mid-summer poll in 2004 found that 50% of European Union citizens saw the United States as playing a negative role "when it comes to preserving peace in the world . . . ," 29% saw it as positive. Interestingly enough, we were more favorably viewed in the new, than the old, EU member states. A Pew Research Center Study in March 2004 showed "an astonishing shift in French and German attitudes toward the U.S. the past two years." In the former, it dropped from 83% to 37%; in the latter from 61% to 38% (Chace, 2004: 17). Not surprisingly, another study reported that "of 35 nations, only three prefer Bush in the coming election, and that on average Kerry is favored 46 percent to 20 percent" (Goldsboroughb, 2004: B-7). And in February 2005 a Pew Research Study found that, around the globe, "anti-Americanism is deeper and broader now than at any time in modern history" (*The Economist*, February 19, 2005: 24).

54. *This Week*, "Bin Laden: Does he want Kerry to win?" (October 8, 2004: 18).

55. In this context, recent works by international scholars argue that the United States would be ill-advised in the long run to "go it alone" in its foreign policy. Indeed, Joseph Nye subtitles his admonition—*Why the World's Only Superpower Can't Go It Alone* (Nye, 2002). See also Daalder and Lindsay (2003); Halper and Clarke (2004); Kagan (2003); Kupchan (2002); Micklethwait and Woodridge (2004); Newhouse (2003); Prestowitz (2003).

56. In a survey taken in 21 nations at the same time as President Bush's second inauguration, 58% thought he "would have a negative impact on peace and security." The responses were negative in 18 of the 21 nations polled. "The survey also indicated that, for the first time, dislike of Mr. Bush translated into a dislike of America in general" (*The Guardian*, January 20, 2004).

Chapter Eight   The Fourth "Whereas"

1. "[T]he cult of ethnicity has arisen both among non-Anglo whites and among nonwhite minorities to denounce the idea of a melting pot, to challenge the concept of 'one people' and to protect, promote and perpetuate separate ethnic and racial communities. . . . [this] does not bode well . . . for the future of the republic" (Schlesinger, 1992: 15, 74) See also Brown et al. (2003), Lareau (2003) and Royster (2003).

2. The budget for the Department of Housing and Urban Development (HUD) has been cut by two-thirds over the past quarter-century (*Atlantic Monthly*, October 2004: 28).

3. See Kotikoff and Burns (2004).

4. "A federal judge in Utah said he reluctantly sentenced a small-time marijuana dealer to 55 years and one day in prison because of harsh mandatory minimums imposed by Congress . . ." *Wall Street Journal* (November 17, 2004: A-5). At the beginning of 2004, there were some 1.5 million men and women in federal and state prisons (2.1% more than the previous year) at an average annual cost of $30,000 plus per prisoner. Of these, 45% were black, 35% white, and 19% Hispanic. The average time being served by inmates has risen from 23 months

in 1995 to 30 months in 2001 and, due to "tougher" sentences, continues to rise. Some 3,300 were on death row. Nearly 10% of all American black males in the age group of 25 to 29 were in prison (*New York Times* News Service, reprinted in *San Diego Union Tribune*, November 8, 2004: A-1, A-12).

5. Up from 19.5% the previous year (*Wall Street Journal*, August 27, 2004: A-1, A-4).

6. "The unmistakable failure of the U.S. health care system has reached a point where proposals for a national solution no longer seem implausible. In its new report on the health care crisis, the National Coalition on Health Care calls for comprehensive, system-wide reform, with mandatory universal coverage. This proposal, coming from an organization that counts among its members some of the largest corporation in the U.S., signals the willingness of some employers to rethink health care issues at a fundamental level" (*LRA ON LINE*, November 26, 2004: 1).

7. To wit: "This week, as President Bush presents his latest budget, half of American cities report they cannot longer provide an 'adequate quantity' of food to those applying for emergency help"(Walker, 2003: 1); and "While the U.S. spends billions of dollars to wage war against Iraq, some 30 million people in the United States go hungry, of whom 12 million are children" (Rizvi, 2003).

8. *Wall Street Journal* (August 27, 2004: A-1, A-4).

9. U.S. Census Bureau (August, 2004).

10. A category referred to, in an earlier, more judgmental era, as the "deserving poor." Although it would require an hourly wage of about $8.85 to meet the aforementioned $18,800 minimum "poverty" level, some 28 million jobs currently fall below this figure (as of early 2005, the minimum hourly wage set by federal law was $5.15.) The data on present-day poverty in the United States, published the day before the third Bush–Kerry debate (announced as focusing on domestic issues, jobs, and the economy), apparently had not come to the attention of the debaters. In all fairness, though, Mr. Kerry was on record as favoring an increase in that wage to $7.00 (*San Diego Union Tribune*, October 12, 2004: C-1, C-5). For more systematic analyses, see Iceland (2003), Alesina and Glaeser (2005).

11. *The Economist* (October 9, 2004: 13). The story went on to report that, in 2000, a Time/CNN survey found that "19% of Americans believed that they were in the top 1% of income earners." (The survey was probably taken in Lake Woebegon, where, as famously reported, all the children are above average, etc.)

12. U.S. Census Bureau (2004: 2).

13. Jordan (2004).

14. *Wall Street Journal* (November 16, 2004: D-3).

15. "With the number of millionaires soaring to more than 2 million in the U.S., the rich are finding it harder to set themselves apart. . . . Today's super-wealthy are creating a whole new category of high end products that are priced beyond the reach of mere millionaires" (Frank, 2004: 1). He then goes on to describe yachts costing "well over $100 million," a sports car "priced at more than $1 million," watches "priced at more than $200,000 and limited edition-watches [that] can now run in the millions."

16. The second half of the book's title, the reader may recall, was *How the American Dream Became the American Fantasy*. The theme is also explored in Cook and

Frank's aptly entitled *Winner Take All Society* (1995). See also the troubling report from the American Political Science Association (2004).

17. Ironically, a case can be made that our top universities "are increasingly rein-forcing rather than reducing these educational inequalities. Poorer students [often suffering from a 'dumbed down' education] are at a huge disadvantage, both when they try to get in and, if they are successful, in their ability to make the most of what is on offer. This disadvantage is most marked in the elite colleges that hold the key to the best jobs" (*The Economist*, January 1, 2005: 24).

18. Perhaps more precisely, those purporting to represent the welfare of the have-nots.

19. And for many, racial or ethnic prejudice.

20. An asset, to be sure, of which they have so far made very little effective use. For a detailed discussion, see the American Political Science Association Task Force Report (2004).

21. By the former in *It Can't Happen Here* (1935), by the latter in *The Plot Against America* (2004).

22. For a top-to-bottom critique, Dahl (2001); for a shorter and more gentle treatment, Lijphart (2000).

23. "Democratic politics is supposed to be about making public arguments and persuading fellow citizens. Instead, it has become an elaborate insider industry in which those skilled at fund-raising, polling, media relations, and advertising have the upper hand" (Dionne, 1991: 332).

24. On the threats created by excessive rates of incumbency victory, see Somit, Wildenmann, and Boll (1994).

25. *This Week*, (October 8, 2004: 18; November 12, 2004: 7). 90% of the incumbents were reelected in both the Senate and the House. Although in the great majority of instances the outcomes are essentially known in advance, cautious donors will often take out insurance by contributing to both sides—though not necessarily with equal generosity.

26. *The Economist* (November 20, 2004: 34). Given the circumstances of their survival, it is not surprising that many politicians "see themselves, despite their assurances otherwise, as being elected primarily to serve the well-to-do" (Simic, 2004: 46).

27. *The Economist* (November 20, 2004: 34).

28. On the role of political party in this dynamic, see Dennis and Owen (2001).

29. We use this term to distinguish those media enterprises that presumably specialize in news from their sister enterprises in radio, television, and publishing whose primary objective is to offer entertainment. We will use the term "media" when we refer to the latter, more inclusive set.

30. The media have also contributed, if inadvertently, to the near-astronomical costs of running for office. Although candidates still make innumerable personal appearances, shake innumerable hands, kiss innumerable infants, and somehow manage to consume innumerable local delicacies, they depend heavily on the media for their appeal to the voter. Getting the message out—via television, radio, newspaper advertising, direct mail, e-mail—requires money, a great deal of it.

31. For what military courts call "charges and specifications," see Fallows (1996). Little seems to have changed—at least in the direction of improvement—over the intervening near decade.

32. His companion contention that "[T]he United States is the only democracy that organizes its national election campaign around the news media" may not be quite a true today as it was then. Patterson (1993: 25).
33. *Atlantic Monthly* (October 2004: 62).
34. To be distinguished from "warm, soft facts" employed by one's adversaries.
35. The usual outcome is some sort of legislative committee hearing that provides a superb opportunity for media spokespersons to testify to the industry's commitment to the highest possible professional standards—and for the Representatives and Senators to voice both their dismay at the deplorable level of programming and their personal devotion to the First Amendment.
36. There is, no doubt, the possibility that the commercial news media might see the "USBC" as relieving them of any further responsibility, let alone need, for upgrading their own news coverage. . . .
37. For excellent discussions, see Havel (1987, 1990); Putnam (1993, 2000); Cook and Frank (1995); and Elshtain (1995).
38. See Patterson (1993); Suskind (2004); Drew (2004); Simic (2004); Elshtain (1995); Crenson and Ginsberg (2002); A.M. Schlesinger (2004); Byrd (2004); Sandel (1996); Tiefer (2004); Hoffman (2004); Todd (2004); Lapham (2004); Goldberg, Goldberg, and Greenwald (2002); Newhouse (2004); Brasch (2005).
39. Somit and Peterson (1997: 109).
40. Among the more recent items: Norgura, 2003; Hess, 2004.
41. Thernstrom and Thernstrom, 2003; Ogbu, 1994, 2003; Lareau, 2003; Brown et al., 2003; Holst, 2004.
42. *This Week*, January 7, 2005: 6.
43. Kronholz, 2004: B-1, B-6.
44. For a recent overview, see Callan (2004). See also Westheimer (2004).
45. Again, see Somit and Peterson, (1997: chapter 9).
46. And see the wide-ranging symposium on the politics of civic education. The introductory essay summarizes the symposium (Westheimer, 2004).

Chapter Nine "Therefore Be It Resolved . . .": Toward More Realistic Foreign and Domestic Policies

1. Generations of doctoral candidates, in search of a dissertation topic, will no doubt be appropriately grateful.
2. For a fuller exposition, see Somit and Peterson (1997: 103–107).
3. President Bush's second inaugural address contained more than a subtle hint that other nations may also be the target of our democratizing efforts.
4. As luck would have it, this was written the day United Nations released a plan to "halve extreme poverty and save the lives of millions of children and hundreds of thousands of mothers by 2015. . . . To fulfill this goal, industrialized nations would need to roughly double aid to poor countries from a quarter to a half of 1 percent of their national incomes." In 2002, the document went on to note, many nations, including the United States, promised to make "concrete efforts" to provide 0.7% of their national incomes for aid to developing countries. The United States currently provides 0.15%, "still the smallest

percentage among donor countries" (*San Diego Tribune*, summarizing a *New York Times* report, January 18, 2005: A-3).

5. The United States now ranks 42nd in infant mortality, worse, for instance, than Cuba. "The problem, most experts agree, is that . . . tens of millions of Americans are trapped in poverty and lack health insurance" *CIA Factbook*, cited in *This Week* (January 28, 2005: 12). The U.S. infant mortality rate rose last year for the first time since 1958.

6. *The Washington Post*, cited in *This Week* (February 18, 2005: 5).

7. Dahlgren (1991: 12).

8. Edsall and Edsall (1991: 257).

9. *The Economist*, December 18 (2004: 44).

10. A process described in literally dozens of novels. For one of the classic examples, see *The Education of Hyman Kaplan* (Rosten, 1937).

11. Most recently by Jared Diamond (2004).

12. For recent differing views, see Modelski (1988) and Lijphart (2000).

References

Acton, Lord. (1877). The history of freedom in antiquity. Address to Members of the Bridgnorth Institute.

Alesina, Alberto and Edward Glaeser. (2004). *Fighting Poverty in the United States and Europe: A World of Difference*. Princeton: Princeton University Press.

Alesina, Alberto and Enrico Spolare. (2004). *The Size of Nations*. Cambridge, MA: MIT Press.

American Political Science Association Task Force on Inequality and American Democracy. (2004). American democracy in an age of rising inequality. *Perspectives on Politics* 2: 651–666.

Anderson, Jon Lee. (2005). A man of the shadows. *The New Yorker* January 24 & 31: 56–59.

Asch, Solomon. (1956). Studies of independence and conformity: A minority of one against a unanimous majority. *Psychological Monographs* 70 (9).

Bachrach, Peter. (1967). *The Theory of Democratic Elitism: A Critique*. Boston: Little, Brown.

Bandow, Doug. (2004). Haiti's requiem for nation-building. www.nationalreview.com/Comment/bandow200403010852.asp.

Banks, Arthur S. (1972). Correlates of democratic performance. *Comparative Politics* 4: 217–230.

Barash, David. (1982). *Sociobiology and Behavior*. New York: Elsevier, 2nd edition.

Barash, David. (1994). State behavior, individual behavior, and the legacy of biology in a troublesome world. *Politics and the Life Sciences* 13: 15–16.

Barkow, Jerome H., Leda Cosmides, and John Tooby (eds.). (1993). *The Adapted Mind*. New York: Oxford University Press.

Barnett, Thomas. (2004). *The Pentagon's New Map*. New York: Penguin.

Barrett, Louise, Robin Dunbar, and John Lycett. (2002). *Human Evolutionary Psychology*. Princeton: Princeton University Press.

Bartov, Omer and Phyllis Mack (eds.). (2002). *In God's Name: Genocide and Religion in the Twentieth Century*. Oxford: Berghahn.

Bauers, K. A. and J. P. Hearn. (1994). Patterns of paternity in relation to male social rank in the stumptailed macaque. *Behaviour* 129: 149–171.

Bell, Daniel. (1961). *The End of Ideology*. New York: Free Press.

Bell, Daniel. (1976). *The Coming of Post-Industrial Society*. New York: Basic Books.

Berman, Carol M. (1986). Maternal lineages as tools for understanding infant social development and social structure. In Richard G. Rawlins and Matt J. Kessler (eds.), *The Cayo Santiago Macaques*. Albany: State University of New York Press.

Bernstein, Irwin S. (1981). Dominance: The baby and the bathwater. *Behavioral and Brain Sciences* 4: 419–429.

Bernstein, Irwin S. (2004). Management of aggression as a component of sociality. In Robert W. Sussman and Audrey R. Chapman (eds.), *The Origins and Nature of Sociality*. Hawthorne, NY: Aldine de Gruyter.

Bernstein, Richard J. (1992). *The New Constellation*. Cambridge, MA: MIT Press.

Bernstein, Richard J. (1993). Postmodernism, dialogue, and democracy. In John Paul Jones III, Wolfgang Natter, and Theodore R. Schatzki (eds.), *Postmodern Contentions*. New York: The Guilford Press.

Boehm, Christopher. (2004). Large-game hunting and the evolution of human sociality. In Robert W. Sussman and Audrey R. Chapman (eds.), *The Origins and Nature of Sociality*. Hawthorne, NY: Aldine de Gruyter.

Brasch, Walter. (2005). *America's Unpatriotic Act*. New York: Peter Lang.

Brecht, Arnold. (1959). *Political Theory*. Princeton: Princeton University Press.

Brown, Donald. (1991). *Human Universals*. New York: McGraw-Hill.

Brown, Michael K. et al. (2003). *Whitewashing Race*. Berkeley, CA: University of California Press.

Brzezinski, Matthew. (2004). *Fortress America: On the Front Lines of Homeland Security*. New York: Bantam Books.

Buruma, Ian and Avishal Margalit. (2004). *Occidentalism: The West in the Eyes of Its Enemies*. New York: Penguin.

Buss, David M. (1999). *Evolutionary Psychology*. Needham Heights, MA: Allyn & Bacon.

Byrd, Robert C. (2004). *Losing America: Confronting a Reckless and Arrogant Presidency*. New York: W. W. Norton.

Cabe, Delia K. (2002). Nation building. www.ksg.harvard.edu/ksgpress/bulletin/Spring2002/features/nation_building.html.

Callan, Eamonn. (2004). *Creating Citizens*. New York: Oxford University Press.

Casper, Gretchen. (1995). *Fragile Democracies*. Pittsburgh: University of Pittsburgh Press.

Casper, Gretchen. (2001). The dynamics of democratization. Presented at American Political Science Association, San Francisco.

Casper, Gretchen and Claudiu Tufis. (2002). Correlation versus interchangeability: The limited robustness of empirical findings on democracy using highly correlated Data sets. *Political Analysis* 11: 1–11.

Cavalieri, P. and Peter Singer. (1993). *The Great Ape Project*. London: Fourth Estate.

Chace, James. (2004). Empire, anyone? *New York Review* October 7: 15–18.

Chase, Marilyn. (2005). Monkeys are willing to "pay" for a glimpse of high-status apes. *Wall Street Journal* February 11: B-5.

Chua, Amy. (2003). *World on Fire: How Exporting Free Market Democracy Breeds Ethnic Hatred*. New York: Doubleday.

Clancy, Tom. (2004). *Battle Ready*. New York: Putnam.

Clarke, Richard A. (2004). *Against All Enemies: Inside America's War on Terror*. New York: Free Press.

Coetzee, J. M. (2003). Awakening. *New York Review* October 23: 4–7.

Cook, Philip J. and Robert H. Frank. (1995). *Winner Take All Society*. New York: Free Press.

Cordesman, Anthony H. (2004). *The War after the War: Strategic Lessons of Iraq and Afghanistan*. Washington, DC: Center for Strategic and International Studies.

Crenson, Matthew and Benjamin Ginsberg. (2002). *Downsizing Democracy: How America Sidelined Its Citizens and Privatized Its Public*. Baltimore: The Johns Hopkins University Press.

Critchley, Simon. (1992). *The Ethics of Deconstruction: Derrida & Levinas*. Oxford: Blackwell Publishers.

Daalder, Ivo and James Lindsay. (2003). *America Unbound: The Bush Revolution in Foreign Policy*. Washington, DC: Brookings Institution Press.

Dahl, Robert A. (1956). *A Preface to Democratic Theory*. Chicago: University of Chicago Press.

Dahl, Robert A. (1960). *Who Governs?* New Haven: Yale University Press.

Dahl, Robert A. (1970). *After the Revolution*. New Haven: Yale University Press.

Dahl, Robert A. (1971). *Polyarchy*. New Haven: Yale University Press.

Dahl, Robert A. (1991). *Modern Political Analysis*. Englewood Cliffs, NJ: Prentice-Hall.

Dahl, Robert A. (1998). *On Democracy*. New Haven: Yale University Press.

Dahl, Robert A. (2001). *How Democratic Is the United States Constitution?* New Haven: Yale University Press.

Dahl, Robert A., Ian Shapiro, and Jose Antonio Cheibub (eds.). (2003). *The Democracy Sourcebook*. Cambridge, MA: MIT Press.

Dahlgren, Peter. (1991). *Communication and Citizenship*. New York: Routledge.

Dahrendorf, Ralf. (1968). *Essays on the Theory of Society*. Stanford, CA: Stanford University Press.

Dalpino, Catharin E. (1998). *Anchoring Third Wave Democracies*. Washington, DC: Institute for the Study of Diplomacy.

Dalpino, Catharin E. (2000). *Deferring Democracy*. Washington, DC: Brookings Institution Press.

Dalton, Russell. (2002). *Citizen Politics*. New York: Chatham House, 3rd edition.

Dalton, Russell J. (2004). *Democratic Challenges, Democratic Choices*. New York: Oxford University Press.

Davis, R. W. (ed.). (1995). *The Origins of Modern Freedom in the West*. Stanford, CA: Stanford University Press, 1995.

Dawkins, Richard. (1989). *The Selfish Gene*. New York: Oxford University Press, Revised edition.

Deak, Istvan. (2002). The crime of the century. *New York Review* September 26: 48–51.

Degler, Carl. (1991). *In Search of Human Nature*. New York: Oxford University Press.

Dempsey, Gary. (2001). The folly of nation-building in Afghanistan. www.cato.org/dailys/10–17–01.html.

Dempsey, Gary. (2002). Old folly in a new disguise. *Policy Analysis* 429, March 21: 1–21.

Dennett, Daniel C. (1995). *Darwin's Dangerous Idea: Evolution and the Meaning of Life*. New York: Simon & Schuster.

Dennis, Jack and Diana Owen. (2001). Popular satisfaction with the party system and representative democracy in the United States. *International Political Science Review* 22: 399–415.

de Ruiter, J. R., Jon A. R. A. M. van Hoof, and W. Scheffrahn. (1993). Social and genetic aspects of paternity in wild long-tailed macaques. *Behaviour* 129: 203–224.

Deutsch, Karl W. (1961). Social mobilization and political development. *American Political Science Review* 55: 493–514.

Diamond, Jared. (2004). *Collapses: How Societies Choose to Fail or Succeed.* New York: Viking.

Diamond, Larry. (2001). Is Pakistan the (reverse) wave of the future? In Larry Diamond and Marc F. Plattner (eds.), *The Global Divergence of Democracies.* Baltimore: The Johns Hopkins University Press.

DiJohn, Jonathan. (2005). Economic liberalization, political instability, and state capacity in Venezuela. *International Political Science Review* 26: 91–106.

Dionne, E. J. (1991). *Why Americans Hate Politics.* New York: Simon & Schuster.

Dixon, William J. (1994). Democracy and the peaceful settlement of international conflict. *American Political Science Review* 88: 14–32.

Dixson, A. F., T. Bossi, and E. J. Wicklings. (1993). Male dominance and genetically determined reproductive success in the mandrill. *Primates* 34: 525–532.

Dobbins, James, John G. McGinn, Keith Crane, Seth G. Jones, Rollie Lal, Andrew Rathmell, Rachel Swanger, and Anga Timilsna. (2003). *America's Role in Nation-Building: From Germany to Iraq.* Santa Monica: RAND.

Dobzhansky, Theodosius. (1951). *Genetics and the Origin of Species.* New York: Columbia University Press.

Donnelly, John. (2003). New democracies face long, hard slog. *San Diego Times-Union* July 25: A-4.

Drew, Elizabeth. (1999). *The Corruption of American Politics: What Went Wrong and Why?* Woodstock, NY: The Overlook Press.

Drew, Elizabeth. (2004). *Fear and Loathing in George W. Bush's Washington.* New York: New York Review Books.

Dryzek, John S. (1990). *Discursive Democracy.* New York: Cambridge University Press.

Dumont, Louis. (1966). *Homo Hierarchicus.* Chicago: University of Chicago Press.

Dunbar, Robin. (1996). *Grooming, Gossip, and the Evolution of Language.* Cambridge, MA: Harvard University Press.

Dunbar, Robin. (2005). Beyond the culture shock. *Nature* January 23: 961–962.

Easton, David. (1956). *A Framework for Political Analysis.* Englewood Cliffs, NJ: Prentice-Hall.

Eaton, G. Gray. (1976). The social order of Japanese macaques. *Scientific American* 235: 97–106.

Edsall, Thomas Byrne and Mary D. Edsall. (1991). *Chain Reaction: The Impact of Race, Rights, and Taxes on American Politics.* New York: W. W. Norton.

Eibl-Eibesfeldt, Irenaus. (1979). Human ethology. *The Behavioral and Brain Sciences* 2: 1–57 (with accompanying commentaries).

Eibl-Eibesfeldt, Irenaus. (1989). *Human Ethology.* New York: Aldine de Gruyter.

Ellis, Lee. (1995). Dominance and reproductive success among nonhuman animals: A cross-species comparison. *Ethology and Sociobiology* 16: 257–333.

Elshtain, Jean Bethke. (1995). *Democracy on Trial.* New York: Basic Books.

Ely, J., P. Alford, and R. E. Ferrell. (1991). DNA "fingerprinting" and the genetic management of a captive chimpanzee population. *American Journal of Primatology* 24: 39–54.

Estes, Richard. (2004). *At the Crossroads: Development Challenges of the New Century.* Dordrecht: Kluwer Academic Publishers.

Fallows, James. (1996). *Breaking the News: How the Media Undermine American Democracy*. New York: Pantheon.

Ferguson, Niall. (2005). To withdraw now would be folly. *Wall Street Journal* February 9: A-10.

Finkel, Steven E. (2002). Civic education and the mobilization of political participation in developing democracies. *Journal of Politics* 4: 994–1020.

Fiorina, Morris P. (2005). *Culture War? The Myth of a Polarized America*. New York: Pearson Longman.

Fox, Jonathan. (2004). Religion and state failure. *International Political Science Review* 25: 55–76.

Fox, Robin. (1989). *The Search for Society*. New Brunswick, NJ: Rutgers University Press.

Frank, Jerome. (1944). Experimental studies of personal pressure and resistance. *Journal of Genetic Psychology* 30: 23–64.

Frank, Robert. (2004). New luxury goods set super wealthy apart from the pack. *Wall Street Journal* December 14: A-1, A-8.

Frank, Robert H. (1985). *Choosing the Right Pond: Human Behavior and the Search for Status*. New York: Oxford University Press.

Fukuyama, Francis. (2004a). Nation-building 101. http://www.theatlantic.com/issues/2004/1/fukuyama.htm.

Fukuyama, Francis. (2004b). *State-Building*. Ithaca, NY: Cornell University Press.

Galbraith, Peter. (2004). How to get out of Iraq. *New York Review*. May 13: 42–46.

Geertz, Clifford. (2003). Which way to Mecca? Part II. *New York Review of Books* July 2: 6.

Gelb, Leslie. (2004). What comes next? *Wall Street Journal* May 20: A-12.

Gerecht, Ruelo Marc. (2004). Ayatollah democracy. *Atlantic Monthly* September: 38–44.

Gill, Graeme D. (2002). *Democracy and Post-Communism: Political Change in the Post-Communist World*. New York: Routledge.

Ginsberg, Benson E. (1988). The evolution of social and political behavior. Presented at American Political Science Association, Washington, DC.

Goldberg, Danny, Victor Goldberg, and Robert Greenwald. (2002). *It's a Free Country: Personal Freedom in America after September 11th*. New York: RDV Books.

Goldsborough, James. (2004a). Haiti's 200 years of hopelessness. *San Diego Union Tribune* March 8: A-14.

Goldsborough, James. (2004b). America is almost alone in the world. *San Diego Union Tribune* September 27: B-7.

Gould, Stephen Jay. (2002). *The Structure of Evolutionary Theory*. Cambridge, MA: Harvard University Press.

Greenberg, Karen J. and Joshua Dratel (eds.). (2005). *The Torture Papers: The Road to Abu Ghraib*. Cambridge: Cambridge University Press.

Greenstein, Fred I. (ed.). (2003). *The George W. Bush Presidency: An Early Assessment*. Baltimore: The Johns Hopkins University Press.

Gurr, Ted Robert, Keith Jaggers, and Will H. Moore. (1991). In Alex Inkeles (ed.), *On Measuring Democracy*. New Brunswick, NJ: Transaction Press.

Gutmann, Amy and Dennis Thompson. (1996). *Democracy and Disagreement*. Cambridge, MA: Harvard University Press.

Habermas, Jurgen. (1975). *Legitimation Crisis*. Boston: Beacon Press (trans. T. McCarthy).

Habermas, Jurgen. (1979). *Communication and the Evolution of Society*. Boston: Beacon Press (trans. T. McCarthy).

Habermas, Jurgen. (1984). *The Theory of Communicative Action, Vol. 1*. Boston: Beacon Press (trans. T. McCarthy).

Hall, K. R. L. and Irven DeVore. (1965). Baboon social behavior. In Irven DeVore (ed.), *Primate Behavior*. New York: Holt, Rinehart, and Winston.

Halper, Stefan and Jonathan Clarke. (2004). *America Alone*. Cambridge: Cambridge University Press.

Harcourt, A. H. and Frans de Waal. (eds.). (1992). *Coalitions and Alliances in Humans and Other Animals*. New York: Oxford University Press.

Hausfater, Glenn, Jeanne Altmann, and Stuart Altmann. (1982). Long-term consistency of dominance relations among female baboons (*Papio Cynocephalus*). *Science* 217: 752–755.

Havel, Vaclav. (1987). *Vaclav Havel, or, Living in Truth*. Boston: Faber & Faber.

Havel, Vaclav. (1990). *Disturbing the Peace*. New York: Alfred A. Knopf.

Held, David. (1993). Democracy: From city-states to a cosmopolitan order? In David Held (ed.), *Prospects for Democracy*. Stanford, CA: Stanford University Press.

Henrich, Joe and Robert Boyd. (1998). The evolution of conformist transmission and the emergence of between-group differences. *Evolution and Human Behavior* 19: 215–242.

Hersh, Seymour. (2004). *Chain of Command: The Road from 9/11 to Abu Ghraib*. New York: Harper Collins.

Hertzberg, Hendrik. (2005). Comment landmarks. *The New Yorker* February 14: 95–98.

Hess, Frederick M. (2004). *Common Sense School Reforms*. New York: Palgrave.

Higgins, Andrew. (2004). Reform in Russia: Free Market, yes; free politics, maybe. *Wall Street Journal* May 23: A-1, A-12.

Hitchens, Christopher. (2004). Reactory prophet. *Atlantic Monthly* April: 130–138.

Hoffman, Stanley. (2004). *Gulliver Unbound: America's Imperial Temptation and the War in Iraq*. New York: Rowman & Littlefield.

Hofling, C. K. et al. (1966). An experimental study of nurse–physician relations. *Journal of Nervous and Mental Disease* 143: 171–180.

Holst, Brad. (2004). Resegregation aftermath. *Atlantic Monthly* July/August: 64.

Huntington, Samuel P. (1991). *The Third Wave*. Norman: University of Oklahoma Press.

Huntington, Samuel P. (1991–1992). How Countries Democratize. *Political Science Quarterly* 106: 579–616.

Iceland, John. (2003). *Poverty in America*. Berkeley, CA: University of California Press.

Ichilov, Orit. (2003). Education and democratic citizenship in a changing world. In David O. Sears, Leonie Huffy, and Robert Jervis (eds.), *Oxford Handbook of Political Psychology*. New York: Oxford University Press.

"Iraq Body Count." (2005). Iraq body count. http://www.iraqbodycount.net/.

Jaffe, Greg. (2004). At the Pentagon, quirky Power Point carries big punch. *Wall Street Journal* May 11: A-1, A-12.

Jennings, Ray Salvatore. (2003). *The Road Ahead: Lessons in Nation-Building from Japan, Germany, and Afghanistan for Postwar Iraq*. Washington, DC: United States Institute of Peace.

Johnson, Diane. (2004). Stiff upper lip. *New York Review* October: 28–29.

Jolly, Alison. (1985). *The Evolution of Primate Behavior*. New York: MacMillan, 2nd edition.

Jordan, Miriam. (2004). Wealth gap widens in U.S. between minorities, whites. *Wall Street Journal* October 18: A-1, A-12.

Judt, Tony. (2003). Israel: The alternative. *New York Review* October 23: 8–10.

Kagan, Robert. (2003). *Of Paradise and Power: America and Europe in the New World Order*. New York: Atlantic Books.

Kamber, Michael. (2005). A troubled Haiti struggles to gain its political balance. *New York Times* January 2: 11.

Kaplan, Robert D. (2004). Five days in Fallujah. *Atlantic Monthly* July/August: 116–126.

Karatynycky, Adam, Aili Piano, and Arch Puddington. (2003). *Freedom in the World 2003: The Annual Survey of Political Rights and Civil Liberties*. New York: Rowman & Littlefield.

Karl, Barry D. (2004). Letter to editor. *Chronicle of Higher Education* February 6: B-18.

Kaufman, Stuart J. (2002). *Modern Hatreds: The Symbolic Politics of Ethnic War*. Ithaca, NY: Cornell University Press.

Kelman, H. C. and V. L. Hamilton. (1989). *Crimes of Authority and Responsibility*. New Haven, CT: Yale University Press.

Kepel, Gilles. (2004). *The War for Muslim Minds: Islam and the West*. New York: Belknap Press.

Key, V. O. (1949). *Southern Politics*. New York: Vintage Books.

Kilham, W. and L. Mann. (1974). Level of destructive obedience as a function of transmitter and executant roles in the Milgram obedience paradigm. *Journal of Personality and Social Psychology* 29: 696–702.

Koford, Carl. (1963). Group relations in an island colony of rhesus macaques. In Charles Southwick (ed.), *Primate Social Relations*. Princeton: D. Van Nostrand.

Kotikoff, Laurence and Scott Burns. (2004). *The Coming Generational Storm: What Should You Know about America's Economic Future*. Cambridge, MA: MIT Press.

Kramer, Jane. (2004). Taking the veil. *The New Yorker* November 22: 59–71.

Kronholz, June. (2004). Economic time bomb: U.S. teens among worst at math. *Wall Street Journal* December 7: B-1, B-6.

Kupchan, Charles A. (2002). *The End of the American Era*. New York: Alfred A. Knopf.

Lapham, Lewis H. (2004). *On the Suppression of Dissent and Stifling of Democracy*. New York: Penguin.

Lareau, Annette. (2003). *Unequal Childhoods, Class, Race, and Family Life*. Berkeley, CA: University of California Press.

Levene, Mark and Penny Roberts (eds.). (1999). *The Massacre in History*. Oxford: Berghahn.

Lewis, Bernard. (2003). I'm right, you're wrong, go to Hell. *Atlantic Monthly* May: 36–42.

Lewis, Sinclair. (1935). *It Can't Happen Here*. New York: Doubleday, Doran & Co.

Lijphart, Arend. (2000). *Democracy in the Twenty-First Century: Can We Be Optimistic?* Wassenaar, The Netherlands: NIAS.

Lipset, Seymour Martin. (1963). *Political Man*. Garden City, NY: Anchor Books.

Lockard, J. S. and D. S. Paulus. (1988). *Self-Deception*. Englewood Cliffs, NJ: Prentice-Hall.

Lomborg, Bjorn. (2004). *Global Crises, Global Solutions*. Cambridge: Cambridge University Press.

McCrone, Donald J. and Charles F. Cnudde. (1967). Toward a communications theory of democratic development. *American Political Science Review* 61: 72–79.

McGrew, W. C. (1991). Chimpanzee material culture: What are its limits and why. In R. A. Foley (ed.), *Origins of Human Behavior*. London: Unwin Hyman.

MacNeill, Allen. (2004). Intelligent design. Posting to evolutionary-psychology@yahoogroups.com. February 22.

"Manifest Destiny . . ." (2003). Manifest destiny warmed up. *The Economist* August 16: 19–21.

Manji, Irshad. (2004). *The Trouble with Islam*. New York: St. Martin's.

Mantell, David M. (1971). The potential for violence in Germany. *Journal of Social Issues* 27: 101–112.

Mara, Gerald M. (2003). Democratic self-criticism and the Other in classical political theory. *Journal of Politics* 65: 739–758.

Marshall, Joshua. (2004). Kerry faces the world. *Atlantic Monthly* July/August: 108–114.

Martin, John et al. (1976). Obedience under conditions demanding self-immolation. *Human Relations* 29: 345–356.

Marx, Karl. (1978). The eighteenth Brumaire of Louis Bonaparte. In Robert C. Tucker (ed.), *The Marx-Engels Reader*. New York: W. W. Norton, 2nd edition (originally published in 1852).

Maynard-Smith, J. (1982). *Evolution and the Theory of Games*. Cambridge: Cambridge University Press.

Mayr, Ernst. (1963). *Animal Species and Evolution*. Cambridge, MA: Harvard University Press.

Mayr, Ernst. (1970). *Populations, Species, and Evolution*. Cambridge, MA: Harvard University Press.

Mayr, Ernst. (1992). Speciational evolution or punctuated equilibria. In Albert Somit and Steven A. Peterson (eds.), *The Dynamics of Evolution*. Ithaca, NY: Cornell University Press.

Mayr, Ernst. (2001). *What Evolution Is*. New York: Basic Books.

Mazur, Allan. (2005). Believer and disbelievers in evolution. Unpublished manuscript.

Meeus, W. H. and Q. A. W. Raaijmakers. (1985). Administrative obedience. Unpublished manuscript cited in Miller (1986).

Meyer-Emerick, Nancy. (2004). Biopolitics, dominance, and critical theory. *Administrative Theory & Praxis* 26: 1–15.

Micklethwait, John and Adrian Woodridge. (2004). *The Right Nation*. New York: Penguin.

Miles, Marc, Edwin Feulner, Mary Anastasia O'Grady, Ana Isabel Eiras, and Aaron Schavey. (2005). *Index of Economic Freedom, 2005*. Washington, DC: Heritage Books.

Milgram, Stanley. (1974). *Obedience to Authority: An Experimental View*. New York: Harper & Row.

Miller, Arthur G. (1986). *The Obedience Experiments*. New York: Praeger.

Modelski, George. (1988). *Is America's Decline Inevitable?* Wassenaar, The Netherlands: NIAS.

Moore, Barrington. (1964). *Social Origins of Dictatorship and Democracy.* Boston: Beacon Press.

Moore, Barrington. (1978). *Inequality: The Social Bases of Obedience and Revolt.* White Plains, NY: M. E. Sharpe.

Mouffe, Chantal. (1993). *The Return of the Political.* London: Verso.

Mouffe, Chantal. (2000). *The Democratic Paradox.* London: Verso.

Moyer, K. E. (1987). The biological basis of dominance and aggression. In Diane McGuinness (ed.), *Dominance, Aggression, and War.* New York: Paragon House.

Muller, Edward N. (1988). Democracy, economic development, and income inequality. *American Sociological Review* 53: 50–68.

Muller, Edward N. and Mitchell A. Seligson. (1994). Civic culture and democracy. *American Political Science Review* 88: 635–652.

Munck, Gerardo L. and Jay Verkullen. (2002). Conceptualizing and measuring democracy: Evaluating alternative indices. *Comparative Political Studies* 35: 5–34.

Myers, B. R. (2004). Mother of all mothers. *Atlantic Monthly* September: 133–142.

Naimark, Norman M. (2001). *Fires of Hatred: Ethnic Cleansing in Twentieth Century Europe.* Cambridge, MA: Harvard University Press.

Nesse, Randolph N. (1994). An evolutionary perspective on substance abuse. *Ethology and Sociobiology* 15: 339–348.

Newhouse, John. (2003). *Imperial America: The Bush Assault on the World Order.* New York: Vintage Books.

Norgura, Pedro. (2003). *City Schools and the American Dream: Reclaiming the Promise of Public Education.* New York: Teachers College Press.

Nye, Joseph S., Jr. (2002). *The Paradox of American Power: Why the World's Only Superpower Can't Go It Alone.* New York: Oxford University Press.

Ober, Josiah. (1993). Public speech and the power of the people in democratic Athens. *PS* 26: 481–486.

Ogbu, John U. with the assistance of Astrid Davis. (2003). *Black American Students in an Affluent Suburb.* Mahwah, NJ: Lawrence Erlbaum Associates.

Ogbu, John U. (1994). *Cultural Models of School Achievement: A Quantitative Test of Ogbu's Theory.* Washington, DC: United States Department of Education, Office of Educational Research and Improvement.

Olson, Steve. (2002). *Mapping Human History: Genes, Race, and Our Common Origins.* Boston: Houghton Mifflin.

Ottaway, Marina. (2004). An effective Iraqi constitution cannot be imposed by fiat. *Chronicle of Higher Education* February 20: B-11.

Packer, C., D. A. Collins, A. Sindimovo, and Jane Goodall. (1995). Reproductive constraints on aggressive competition in female baboons. *Nature* 373: 60–63.

Pagels, Elaine. (1979). *The Gnostic Gospels.* New York: Random House.

Paris, Roland. (2004). *At War's End: Building Peace after Civil Conflict.* Cambridge: Cambridge University Press.

Pateman, Carole. (1970). *Participation and Democratic Theory.* New York: Cambridge University Press.

Patterson, Thomas. (1993). *Out of Order.* New York: Alfred A. Knopf.

Patterson, Thomas. (2002). *The Vanishing Voter.* New York: Alfred A. Knopf.

Paul, A. and J. Kuester. (1990). Adaptive significance of sex ratio adjustment in semifree-ranging Barbary macaques at Salem. *Behavioral Ecology and Sociobiology* 27: 287–293.

Pei, Minxin and Sara Kasper. (2003). Lessons from the past: The American record on nation-building. Carnegie Endowment for International Piece. Briefing paper # 24, May.

Peterson, Steven A. (2002). Reification, hegemony, and the human brain. In Gerald A. Cory, Jr. and Russell Gardner (eds.), *The Evolutionary Neuroethology of Paul MacLean*. Westport, CT: Greenwood.

Peterson, Steven A. (in press). Evolution, cognition, and decision-making. In Göktug Morçöl (ed.), *Handbook of Decision-Making*. New York: Marcel Dekker.

Pharr, Susan J., Robert D. Putnam, and Russell J. Dalton. (2001). A quarter-century of declining confidence. In Larry Diamond and Marc F. Plattner (eds.), *The Global Divergence of Democracies*. Baltimore: The Johns Hopkins University Press.

Phillips, Kevin. (1990). *Politics of Rich and Poor*. New York: Random House.

Pinker, Steven. (2002). *The Blank Slate: The Modern Denial of Human Nature*. New York: Viking.

Plano, Jack and Milton Greenberg. (1993). *The American Political Dictionary*. Fort Worth: Harcourt Brace Jovanovich, 9th edition.

Popper, Karl. (1962). *The Open Society and Its Enemies*. London: Routledge and Kegan Paul.

Power, Samantha. (2004). The lesson of Hannah Arendt. *New York Review of Books* April 29: 34–37.

Premack, David. (1988). "Does the chimpanzee have a theory of mind" revisited. In Richard W. Byrne and Andrew Whiten (eds.), *Machiavellian Intelligence*. Oxford: Clarendon Press.

Prestowitz, Clyde. (2003). *Rogue Nation: American Unilateralism and the Failure of Good Intentions*. New York: Basic Books.

Przeworski, Adam. (1999). Minimalist conception of democracy: A defense. In Ian Shapiro and Casiano Hacker-Cordon (eds.), *Democracy's Value*. Cambridge: Cambridge University Press.

Przeworski, Adam, Michael E. Alvarez, Jose Antonio Cheibub, and Dernando Limongi. (2001). What makes democracies endure? In Larry Diamond and Marc F. Plattner (eds.), *The Global Divergence of Democracies*. Baltimore: The Johns Hopkins University Press.

Putnam, Robert. (1993). *Making Democracy Work: Civic Traditions in Modern Italy*. Princeton: Princeton University Press.

Putnam, Robert. (2000). *Bowling Alone*. New York: Simon & Schuster.

Rank, S. G. and C. K. Jacobson. (1977). Hospital nurses' compliance with medication overdose orders. *Journal of Health and Social Behavior* 18: 188–193.

Rauf, Feisal Abdul. (2004). *What's Right with Islam?* New York: Harper.

Ray, George R. (2004). AR 15–6. Investigation of the Abu Ghraib Detention Facility and 205 Military Intelligence Brigade.

Reporters without Borders. (2003). U. S. Ranked 31st. www.rsf.com.

Ridley, Matt. (1994). *The Red Queen*. New York: Viking.

Rizvi, Haider. (2003). Hungry in a wealthy nation. *Global Policy Forum* March 26. http://www.globalpolicy.org/socecon/develop/2003/0326ushunger.htm.

Rose, David. (2004). *Guantanamo: The War on Human Rights*. New York: New Press.

Rosett, Claudia. (2004). Against "nation-building." www.opinionjournal.com/columnists/cRosett/?id=95001222.

Rosten, Leo. (1937). *Education of Hyman Kaplan*. New York: Harcourt, Brace.

Roth, Philip. (2004). *The Plot Against America*. New York: Houghton Mifflin.

Royster, Deidre. (2003). *Race and the Invisible Hand*. Berkeley, CA: University of California Press.

Rubin, Paul H. (2002). *Darwinian Politics: The Evolutionary Origins of Freedom*. New Brunswick, NJ: Rutgers University Press.

Rumsfeld, Donald H. (2003). Beyond "nation-building." *Washington Post* September 25: A-33.

Russett, Bruce. (1993). *Grasping the Democratic Peace*. Princeton: Princeton University Press.

Russett, Bruce and William Antholis. (1992). Do democracies rarely fight each other? Evidence from the Peloponnesian War. *Journal of Peace Research* 29: 415–434.

Sagan, Carl and Ann Druyan. (1992). *Shadows of Forgotten Ancestors*. New York: Ballantine Books.

Samuelson, Robert J. (1996). *The Age of Entitlement: How the American Dream Became the American Fantasy*. New York: Random House.

Sandel, Michael. (1996). *Democracy's Discontent*. Cambridge, MA: Harvard University Press.

Sanin, Francesco Gutierrez. (2005). Fragile democracy and schizophrenic liberalism: Exit, voice and loyalty in the Andes. *International Political Science Review* 26: 125–140.

Schedler, Andreas. (2001). "What Is Democratic Consolidation?" In Larry Diamond and Marc F. Plattner (eds.), *The Global Divergence of Democracies*. Baltimore: The Johns Hopkins University Press.

Schlesinger, Arthur M., Jr. (1992). *The Disuniting of America*. New York: W. W. Norton.

Schlesinger, Arthur M., Jr. (2004). *War and the American Presidency*. New York: W. W. Norton.

Schlesinger, James R. et al. (2004). *Final Report of the Independent Panel: Review of Department of Defense Operations*.

Schumpeter, Joseph. (1975). *Capitalism, Socialism, and Democracy*. New York: Harper & Row.

Schwartz, Peter H. (1989). "His Majesty the baby": Narcissism and royal authority. *Political Theory* 17: 266–290.

Schwartzberg, Melissa. (2004). Athenian democracy and legal change. *American Political Science Review* 98: 311–324.

Shanab, M. E. and K. A. Yahya. (1978). A cross-cultural study of obedience. *Bulletin of the Psychonomic Society* 11: 267–269.

Shepher, Joseph. (1987). Commentary. In Diane McGuinness (ed.), *Dominance, Aggression*. New York: Paragon.

Sheridan, C. L. and R. G. King. (1972). Obedience to authority with an authentic victim. *Proceedings of the American Psychological Association* 1972: 156–166.

Sherif, Muzafer. (1936). *The Psychology of Social Norms*. New York: Harper & Row.

Shipler, David K. (2004). *The Working Poor: Invisible in America*. New York: Alfred A. Knopf.

Simic, Charles. (2004). Down there on a visit. *New York Review* August 12: 45–47.

Simon, Herbert. (1990). A mechanism for social selection and successful altruism. *Science* 250: 1666–1668.

Simpson, George Gaylord. (1944). *Tempo and Mode*. New York: Columbia University Press.

Simpson, George Gaylord. (1953). *The Major Features of Evolution*. New York: Columbia University Press.

Skocpol, Theda. (2004). *Diminished Democracy: From Membership to Management in American Civic Life*. Norman: University of Oklahoma Press.

Smith, D. G. (1993). A 15-year study of the association between dominance rank and reproductive success of male rhesus macaques. *Primates* 34: 471–480.

Somit, Albert and Steven A. Peterson. (1997). *Darwinism, Dominance, and Democracy* Greenwich, CT: Praeger.

Somit, Albert and Steven A. Peterson (eds.). (2003). *Human Nature and Public Policy*. New York: Palgrave MacMillan.

Somit, Albert, Rudolf Wildenmann, and Bernhard Boll. (1994). *The Victorious Incumbent: A Threat to Democracy?* Dartmouth: Dartmouth Publishing.

Sontag, Deborah and Lydia Polgreen. (2004). Storm-battered Haiti's endless crises deepen. *The New York Times* October 16: A-1, A-5.

Stael, Ronald. (2004). George Kennan at 100. *New York Review of Books* April 29: 8–9.

Stanford, Craig. (2001). *Significant Others*. New York: Basic Books.

Staub, Ervin. (1989). *The Roots of Evil: The Origins of Genocide and Other Group Violence*. New York: Cambridge University Press.

Stayton, D. J., R. Hogan, and M. D. Ainsworth. (1971). Infant obedience and maternal behavior: The origins of socialization reconsidered. *Child Development* 42: 1057–1069.

Stewart, Kelly J. and Alexander H. Harcourt. (1987). Gorillas: Variation in female relationships. In Barbara Smuts et al. (eds.), *Primate Societies*. Chicago: University of Chicago Press.

Stimson, James A. (2004). *Tides of Consent: How Public Opinion Shapes American Politics*. Cambridge: Cambridge University Press.

Stonjek, Robert. (2004). The religious instinct is biologically a tribal war instinct? (Tables). Posting to evolutionary-psychology@yahoogroups.com. September 6.

Students for a Democratic Society. (1985). Port Huron statement. In Alpheus T. Mason and Gordon Baker (eds.), *Free Government in the Making*. New York: Oxford University Press.

Summers, Kyle. (2005). The evolutionary ecology of despotism. *Evolution and Human Behavior* 26: 106–135.

Suskind, Ron. (2004). *The Price of Loyalty: George W. Bush, the White House, and the Education of Paul O'Neill*. New York: Simon & Schuster.

Tattersall, Ian. (2002). *The Monkey in the Mirror*. New York: Harcourt.

Teachout, Terry. (2003). *The Skeptic: H. L. Mencken*. New York: Harper Collins.

Thayer, Bradley. (2004). *Darwin and International Relations*. Lexington, KY: The University Press of Kentucky.

Thernstrom, Abigail and Stephen Thernstrom. (2003). *No Excuses: Closing the Racial Gap In Learning*. New York: Simon & Schuster.

Thierry, B. (2000). Covariation of conflict management patterns across macaque species. In F. Aureli and Frans B. M. de Waal (eds.), *Natural Conflict Resolution* Berkeley, CA: University of California Press.

Tiefer, Charles. (2004). *Veering Right—Bush Administration Subverts the Law.* Berkeley, CA: University of California Press.

Tiger, Lionel. (1992). *The Pursuit of Pleasure.* Boston: Little, Brown.

Tiger, Lionel and Robin Fox. (1971). *The Imperial Animal.* New York: Dell.

Todd, Emmanuel. (2004). *After the Empire: The Breakdown of the American Order.* New York: Columbia University Press.

Trivers, Robert. (1971). The evolution of reciprocal altruism. *Quarterly Review of Biology* 46: 35–57.

Tuchman, Barbara. (1981). *The Meaning of History.* New York: Alfred A. Knopf.

United Nations Development Programme. (2002). *Deepening Democracy in a Fragmented World.* New York: United Nations Development Programme.

Urquhart, Brian. (2003). World order & Mr. Bush. *New York Review* October 9: 8–12.

van der Molen, P. P. (1990). The biological instability of social equilibria. In Johan van der Dennen and Vincent Falger (eds.), *Sociobiology and Conflict.* London: Chapman and Hall.

Vanhanen, Tatu. (1984). *The Emergence of Democracy.* Helsinki: Finnish Society of Sciences and Letters.

Vanhanen, Tatu. (1990). *The Process of Democratization.* New York: Crane Russak.

Vanhanen, Tatu. (2003). *Democratization: A Comparative Analysis of 170 Countries.* London: Routledge.

Vicenzo, Marco. (2004). International community must act to stabilize Haiti. *The San Diego Union-Tribune* March 7, 2004: G-6.

Vidal, Dominique. (2003). Reconstructing states: A guide to nation-building. *La Monde Diplomatique*, December. http://mondediplo.com/2003/12/10rand.

Waal, Frans de. (1989). *Peacemaking among Primates.* Cambridge, MA: Harvard University Press.

Wade, Robert Hunter. (2005). Failing states and cumulative causation in the world system. *International Political Science Review* 26: 17–36.

Walker, David. (2003). Down and out in America. *Guardian* February 2: 1.

Walters, Jeffrey R. and Robert M. Seyfarth. (1987). Conflict and cooperation. In Barbara Smuts et al. (eds.), *Primate Societies.* Chicago: University of Chicago Press.

Wantchekon, Leonard. (2004). The paradox of warlord democracy: A theoretical investigation. *American Political Science Review* 98: 17–33.

Watanabe, John M. and Barbara Smuts. (2004). Cooperation, commitment, and communication in the evolution of human sociality. In Robert W. Sussman and Audrey R. Chapman (eds.), *The Origins and Nature of Sociality.* Hawthorne, NY: Aldine de Gruyter.

Westheimer, Joel. (2004). Introduction—the politics of civic education. *PS* 37: 231–234.

White, Stephen K. (1991). *Political Theory and Postmodernism.* New York: Cambridge University Press.

"Whose Coup . . ." (2004). Whose coup in Haiti? *The Economist* March 6: 13–14.

Wilkinson, Rupert. (1969). *Governing Elites: Studies in Training and Selection.* Oxford: Oxford University Press.

Williams, George. (1966). *Adaptation and Natural Selection* Princeton, NJ: Princeton University Press.

Wilson, David Sloan. (1995). Group selection and human ethology. *Human Ethology Bulletin* 10 (3): 2–4.

Wilson, David Sloan. (2002). *Darwin's Cathedral: Evolution, Religion, and the Nature of Society.* Chicago: University of Chicago Press.

Wilson, David Sloan and Elliott Sober. (1994). Reintroducing group selection to the human behavioral sciences. *Behavioral and Brain Sciences* 17: 585–654 (with accompanying commentaries).

Wilson, Edward O. (1975) *Sociobiology.* Cambridge, MA: Harvard University Press.

Wright, Robert. (1994). *The Moral Animal.* New York: Vintage Books.

Zakaria, Fareed. (2004). *The Future of Freedom.* New York: W. W. Norton.

Name Index

Subject Index

Abu Ghraib, 91, 113
Adaptations, 10
Afghanistan, xi, 7, 8, 36, 39, 40, 44, 48, 49, 52, 54, 55, 57–60, 77, 81, 82, 83, 84, 86, 87, 89, 90–91, 113, 117, 123, 129
Africa, 49, 55, 63
Age of Democracy, xi, 2, 6, 21, 93
American Political Science Association, xiii
Angola, 40
Armenia, 74
Athens, 20, 61–62, 97, 123, 126
Australia, 91
Authoritarianism, 1, 2, 3, 4, 5, 9, 47, 51–52, 54, 55, 77, 112, 118, 124
Azerbaijan, 74

Bahamas, 71
Balkans, 71
Belarus, 74
Belgium, 62, 125
Bosnia-Herzogovina, 36, 40, 71, 125
British Broadcasting Corporation (BBC), 104
British Journal of Political Science, xiii

Cambodia, 40
Canada, 62
Casualties, Americans in Afghanistan, 86
Casualties, Americans in Iraq, 86
Central Intelligence Agency, 52, 135
"Chattering classes," 103, 106, 124

Chechnya, 129
Check list, decisional, 6, 47–60, 11–112
Check list, operational, 6, 39–40, 45–46, 58–60, 84, 111–112
China, 127, 130
Civic education, 94, 106–109, 113, 115
Civil liberties, 88, 122
Criminal justice system, 89, 94, 131–132
Culture, 21, 119
Czechoslovakia, 115
Czech Republic, 72

Darwinian theory, xi, 5, 9–23, 112
Darwinism, Dominance, and Democracy, xi
Democracy, xi, 1, 2, 3, 4, 5, 20–22, 24–33, 53, 56, 60, 61–75, 80, 90, 92, 93, 97, 115, 116, 117, 118, 121, 124, 130, 132
Democracy, participatory, 26–28, 121
Democratic citizenship, education for, 7
Dominance, 11–20, 119
Dominican Republic, 73, 108

East Timor, 125
The Economist, 55, 63, 97, 100, 123, 124, 130
Elections, 7, 25, 26, 28, 30, 31, 32, 36, 42, 43, 63, 83–84, 88, 89, 99, 125, 130
El Salvador, 124
England, 53; *see also* Great Britain
Eritrea, 72